BYTES 0

EVOLVING LEADERSHIP FOR THE SPIRITUAL ENTREPRENEUR

ANGEL ROHRER ~ SETH ROHRER

FEATURING: JORGE LUIS DELGADO, LAURA DI FRANCO,
KRISTINA DUBOIS, KYA DUBOIS, JENNIFER FALCHI, RACHELLE GOLDING,
ELIZA JAMES, GURPREET JUNEJA, APRIL KAISER, DUSTIN KAISER,
GRACE KOHN, EMOKE MOLNAR, DAPHNE PARAS, SUZANNE ROLLEN,
GRACE SOLARIS, BRADFORD W. TILDEN, ATLANTIS WOLF

FOREWORD BY LEE McCORMICK, AUTHOR OF *THE HEART RECONNECTION GUIDEBOOK*

BYTES OF LIGHT

EVOLVING LEADERSHIP FOR THE SPIRITUAL ENTREPRENEUR

ANGEL ROHRER ~ SETH ROHRER

FEATURING: JORGE LUIS DELGADO, LAURA DI FRANCO,
KRISTINA DUBOIS, KYA DUBOIS, JENNIFER FALCHI, RACHELLE GOLDING,
ELIZA JAMES, GURPREET JUNEJA, APRIL KAISER, DUSTIN KAISER,
GRACE KOHN, EMOKE MOLNAR, DAPHNE PARAS, SUZANNE ROLLEN,
GRACE SOLARIS, BRADFORD W. TILDEN, ATLANTIS WOLF

FOREWORD BY LEE MCCORMICK, AUTHOR OF *THE HEART RECONNECTION GUIDEBOOK*

ENDORSEMENTS

This book contains a refreshing collection of voices that reflect the raw authenticity and empowered vulnerability required to walk the path of true spirituality—where the divine is revealed within the human experience and without the separation of hierarchical worship. God has been called out from the enigma of the 'guru' and into the hearts of familiar faces and 'ordinary' stories made extraordinary by their earnest embrace of love. It's this god-next-door mentality that will walk us all home to our divine residence within.

~ Rebecca Haywood, Nagual healer, mentor, and contributing author of *Shamanism in the New Millennium* and *Dancing in the Unknown*

Angel and Seth have created a beautiful dream with the intent of sharing the wisdom from their hearts to help people to transform and open their hearts. In this book my Inca teacher, Don Jorge Delgado, and my boxing sensei Eliza James, and other spiritual messengers of love and light have been invited to contribute as a Wolfpack of light to guide you on a path of self-awareness to live life with love, respect, and gratitude!"

~ Don Jose Ruiz, Toltec Nagual, New York Times Bestselling Author of *The 5th Agreement* and *Shamanic Power Animals*

"Angel Rohrer has put together a compendium of explorations that will take you on a wild and inspirational journey, a deep dive into the revelations and insights that can come from a willingness to open yourself to Spirit and provide guidance for your soul's path."

~ Dr. Steven Farmer, Psychotherapist, shamanic practitioner, and bestselling author of *Earth Magic* and *Animal Spirit Guides*

In a world faced with what seems like insurmountable change, an entirely new form of leadership is required. You'll find the innovation and inspiration you need in Bytes of Light. Angel and Seth Rohrer tenderly and skillfully compel you to consider a rich, purpose-driven, deeply potent form of leadership – the kind of leadership that emerges from the fearless yet vulnerable exploration of your own soul. Commit yourself to this medicine, and you'll not only heal yourself, you will also lead the world to healing!

~Dr. Ahriana Platten – Bestselling Author of
Rites and Rituals – Harnessing the Power of Sacred Ceremony.

I am so honored to have walked with you on your path, Angel. As you know, I do not believe in coincidence, and I know it was simply what was required to move forward. The team still talks about all the amazing experiences, growth, and learning we had because of your time with us. Thank you for continuing to bring the light!

~ Dr. Raeleen Manjak, DM/OL, ΔMΔ, CPHR

Bytes of Light is a gift and sacred longing answered. Powerful stories and words that weave wisdom from the embodied feminine and masculine leadership emerging in the world today.

~ Stephanie Urbina Jones, #1 Billboard Country Music Songwriter,
dreamer, and artist of life

Bytes of Light

Evolving Leadership for the Spiritual Entrepreneur

Angel Rohrer and Seth Rohrer

©Copyright 2023 Rohrer Revolution LLC

Published by Brave Healer Productions

Paperback ISBN: 978-1-961493-07-0

eBook ISBN: 978-1-961493-08-7

FOREWORD
OUR PATH BACK HOME

BEING BORN INTO THIS WORLD IS NOT FOR THE FAINT OF HEART

Our human legacy has become extremely complicated. We inherit multiple layers of energies, imprints, memories, stories, beliefs, and legacies. We are domesticated to live by the books of rules and laws of our cultures, religions, families, neighborhoods, and greater cultures. This is our human indoctrination if you will.

There is an unspoken side to all these layers of influence that's often not directly addressed and that's a silent assumption that we were not born of inherent goodness and value. That who we are as unique, creative, divine expressions of life can only realize value by giving our faith away to the rules and institutions of our birthplaces as we earn value according to the world of man.

Only by living up to the external expectations of this world of man might we redeem ourselves as valuable based on the conditions and judgments we were born into.

We each inherit our little piece of this action, as I like to refer to it. No judgment is needed. It is what it is and yes, it can be very overwhelming to the hearts and souls of those of us who land here on Earth.

Our inherited situation is not personal. We each have inherited our unique piece of this great living puzzle and we each have our unique gifts and aspects of spirit and soul hidden within that can be, should we be so fortunate to realize, our bytes of light to guide us on our journey.

Ancient human mystery schools realized this challenging human situation thousands of years ago. Mystery schools provided an interface between the realms of Spirit, multidimensionality, and human legacy—mind/emotions/spirit, magic, transformation, and alchemy.

Over the last thousand years or so humanities cultures moved away from the mystery school ways to a more rigid, defined 'left' brained interpretation of life. We chose our ideas of control and science as the definers of life and possibilities.

We gave our faith to our own made-up beliefs of reality as we sought safety from the unknown. In a sense we put ourselves on an island of our own creation separating our mystical self from our analytical self, turning away from our mystic for the false security of our 'known' beliefs.

This has been the primary operating system we humans have lived with for a long, long time now. If you look at it free from judgment or attachment it is an interesting path we have lived to get to this point.

Ahhhh, but now it seems the cows have come home, the well-endowed lady is singing, the tide has turned and we are up to our ears in self-perpetuated challenges both personally and collectively. Challenges and sufferings can be viewed as a curse or as a blessing. How could suffering be a blessing? It is our sufferings that call our attention back to this moment, this now, this only place we can use our will and attention to decide if it is time for a change. As always it is a matter of choice and point of view.

As we begin to wake up to our 'reality,' we face some great invitations to look in life's mirrors. After all we are each 100% responsible for the personal reality we have created and we still hold the power to re-create our relationships, beliefs, patterns, and identities based now on our present moment awareness and inspirations.

WE CAN LEARN TO SHED THE SKINS OF BEING VICTIMS TO LIFE AND THIS WORLD, IF WE CHOOSE TO.

We can unravel and let go of the heavy energies we have chosen to carry as our stories and identities. We can release the old legacies that have haunted us for generations. We can recreate all our relationships, which must begin with ourselves.

Bytes of Light are glimpses into the lives of an array of individuals who have said yes to this call to wake up.

As human beings we have amazing gifts as storytellers. Our stories hold the potential to become aspects of our medicines in healing and evolving beyond the shade we once cast on our home here on Earth.

As we step up and out into the light of a new way of being, we are also stepping onto that path of the heart that can lead us back home to ourselves. Leading us to our true uncompromised and untouched soul self that has been patiently waiting for generations for these moments to arrive.

We are the ones we have been waiting for.

We are the BYTES OF LIGHT that will illuminate the path ahead.

May you be inspired as you read this book,

may you be inspired to step up in your life,

to come home to the spark of magic and divinity

that has always been the truth of your incarnation

in this fantastic world of dreams.

Welcome Home. ONWARD

Lee McCormick- Author, *The Heart Reconnection Guidebook*

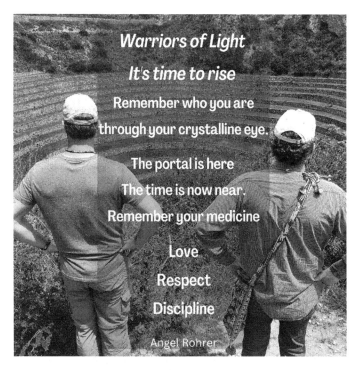

Warriors of Light

It's time to rise

Remember who you are
through your crystalline eye.

The portal is here
The time is now near.

Remember your medicine

Love

Respect

Discipline

Angel Rohrer

NOTE TO YOU COURAGEOUS READERS

ASCENSION SYMPTOMS ARE A THING

So, you pick up this book and binge the whole thing and are now finding yourself setting up camp in the bathroom because your body is going through a full detox in unimaginable ways, and you don't know what the hell is happening!

WELCOME TO THE "ASCENSION DETOX CLUB"

The common Canadian phrase, "Does a bear shit in the woods?" became a reality in my world after an intense power journey in Teotihuacan, Mexico, as I made my way home and had to drive through the Rocky Mountains with no bathrooms along the highway. If you want full glorious details with lots of laughs, head over to our Bytes of Light Podcast and watch Episode 4.

Nobody escapes unscathed. The cool thing is that everyone experiences ascension symptoms differently, as we all came onto this planet with different ancestral programming. I can provide you with a list of things that may happen, so you are aware. If these things are happening to you, know it's an integral part of the process.

Physically, our body holds cellular memory. When we choose to shift habits, patterns, and own our wounds and stories, our bodies will act physically as if in danger, they are sick, or feel like they will die.

NOTICE, I SAY OUR BODIES ACT THAT WAY

We are choosing to shift our attention and awareness, so our conscious brains understand we are willingly choosing to go on this ride. This does not mean our bodies will be able to keep up with the rate we are loading light into our systems.

Bingeing this book would be the same as sitting out in the direct sun with no sunscreen or shade. It would amount to incoming burns and heat stroke for some, while others may be simply fine. It all depends on your level of awareness and if some of the stories trigger you or not. The level of commitment you bring to your own personal growth will correlate with your level of ascension and the number of symptoms you experience. Slow and steady, always stay with yourself and honor where you are at in every moment. Self-care is your best friend!

IT TAKES THE ENERGY OF A WARRIOR TO SHIFT OUR CONSCIOUSNESS INTO THE LIGHT

Know we are honored by you reading our permeated words of light and are here for you when you have questions or want more information. You are never alone on this journey.

We have built a private Facebook Group to assist you. You can bring your questions to all the authors in this collaboration; we will all be there to guide you to your highest truth.

Welcome to our Den of Light,
where you will be held and honored
for facing your fears, owning your power,
and standing tall on your two pillars of light, we humans call legs.

Get access to The Bytes of Light Community Facebook Group here: https://www.facebook.com/groups/169323216970027

For ascension symptoms guideline, follow this link: https://www.rohrerrevolution.com/ascension-symptoms-guide

Stardust falls from the sky

I'm sitting on the moon

I hear the call from humanity,

I know I must go soon

Growling as my paws

Land on earthen floor

Fur and claws

Fangs and blood,

Gaia welcomes me to the hood

Where are you?

I see you up in blue

Howling, the lonely

Call of the Wolf

My soul calls out to you

Stillness, darkness,

must find my vision.

Severing throats of those

on a dark mission

Why am I here?

What does my soul crave this time?

My new furry soul basket

Lets out a small whine

As I look into the stars and ask for a sign.

"Remember who you are little one,

this next trip to Earth

I promise, will be divine."

Nestling in my den

Among my brethren

Protected and held

while I heal deep within

The sacred Feminine

This is my medicine

Medicine of the Wolf

-Willow White Wolf

DREAMING WITH WILLOW WHITE WOLF

I vividly remember taking my beautiful white husky for a walk daily as a child. Children will categorize things they learn in the structures they have already been domesticated with, and in my tiny little world, this imaginary pet I had was indeed a dog.

Most humans I've conversed with in this world had imaginary human friends. Mine showed up in fur form and my earliest remembrance was of this huge, beautiful, white dog.

Walking down the sidewalk with my hand resting on the powerful shoulder blades of this magnificent creature, for me, it was as real as the sun shining on my face.

It was not until I was in my teens that I saw a picture of a white wolf and made the connection; my dog was not a husky. It was a wolf. This realization opened magical portals of possibilities I chose to go down. How did I know what a wolf looked like as a small child, without ever seeing one? This question had me seeking answers the humans surrounding me did not have answers for.

When you ask the Universe to show you signs, they show up in ways you do not see coming, and in 2013, a human showed up in my world with deep wolf medicine to share.

I was facilitating at a private drug and alcohol retreat center, nestled in the Kootenay mountains, where part of the medicine is a weekly sweat lodge on an indigenous reserve with its elders. This man had an experience where he could not breathe through the intense heat and was about to ask to leave the lodge when a wolf curled up to his chest and breathed cool air into his mouth as she laid with him. Upon telling this experience to me, he shared that he had been raising two wolf cubs from eight weeks old and they were a year old now. The little female, Willow, came to him in the sweat lodge.

A month later, he took me to another province where the wolves were being cared for, only to discover they were both shot and killed for their pelts during that brief time he was away in recovery by the indigenous on the reserve next to them.

The ruthless realization hit like an atomic bomb. Willow was already dead when she came to visit him in the sweat lodge. River, on the other hand, ran after he witnessed his sister being killed. He covered hundreds of kilometers before being shot in a farmer's field and ending his journey on Earth this round as well.

With my attunement to wolf medicine, and his experience with these baby wolves' short lives, we chose to take on their names in honor of their impactful journey in our lives, and Willow White Wolf was born within.

Wolves mate for life.

After half a dozen years, when one partner chooses a different life and kills the storyline, how does the other move on?

How does the whole pack move on without the alpha male?

Oh wait.

Are 'alpha' and 'male' the only two words that go together? What about alpha female?

What does alpha mean?

What is the opposite and where do I fit into the mix?

As a human with a female soul basket?

These questions had me digging into the depths of my soul for this last decade. *Who am I, and how do I want to show up in this world at this unprecedented time on earth?*

We are experiencing a quantum shift on this planet, where the patriarchal ways are being dismantled as Mama Gaia says "no" to some of the behaviors happening here on Earth. We are all being asked to look internally and challenge the agreements we have been domesticated with, and make better, more informed choices moving forward.

But how? We know things need to change, both internally and externally. The question is, where do we start?

In my Toltec Shamanic apprenticeship, we spent years unraveling the concepts of 'power over versus power within' and the subtleties of control and manipulation within relationships. This has been great medicine as the world experiences the shift of us humans leaning more into the divine feminine aspects of who we are and what that looks like.

As I experimented with these energies, it became clear I was born with a generous capacity to feel and see subtle energies, however those abilities were suppressed by my environment and lack of knowledge as a child. The divine masculine within prevailed and I made my way through life with a warrior's heart and chose leadership as my form of communication and community.

As I dove deeper into the underworld, the shadow aspect of myself and my ancestral lineage, I surrendered to the goddess within, forgave myself for all the mistakes I made along this journey, forgave those who harmed me, and vowed to listen deeper to my soul, knowing there was more medicine within. Three years ago, I committed to the Ruiz family in an intense apprenticeship and gave them permission to 'train Willow.' This feral aspect inside me was full of fire, which I had no control over, and she needed puppy training.

She had been hurt, abused, abandoned, and almost killed. She needed help, and to heal her, I had to ask my warrior to put her sword down, surrender, forget all I had known, and allow these healers to assess and give me the experiences I needed to awaken the goddess within.

Three men. What a concept. How did these men teach me the goddess way?

Energetic agility is the secret sauce

to keep authenticity alive in modernized gender roles.

Agility means you are skilled in both alpha and omega, and can pivot between the two embodiments at will, choosing whichever best serves the moment.

Rather than seeing these aspects as something fixed, you see them as a dance that occurs from moment to moment, each partner feeling into the situation and deciding which aspect to offer based on what would best serve the moment.

To train yourself to move between alpha and omega takes practice, no doubt, and in my experience, I needed healers who could "out alpha me" so I could lean in and strengthen my goddess spiritual muscles, knowing I was safe and held.

It takes advanced awareness to know which aspect you are occupying and what is needed within the relationship in question. This is where true authentic leadership is born. You can only teach to the level of what you embody on both sides.

It takes practice to master the capacity to switch aspects on the fly.

My wish for humanity is to understand this sacred dance of the divine feminine and masculine aspects within. Ignite the passion for oneness by diving into your own heart to discover you truly are the love of your life. You can create your own safety, be your own warrior, as well as nurture the creative oracle that births magic into this world. We are both; we house both and all things. Our energy connects to all things on this planet because we are all one.

As you start to embody these energies and heighten your awareness, humans that can match and dance this agile dance as well will start to show up in your world to play with. That, my loves, is why we are here!

Let us dive into the mystery together and allow our puppies to play!

The Seed. That which blooms and blossoms all life force. It centers and grounds our wolf in sacred presence. Our wolf, a young pup ready and yearning to run wild, without present thought, living out of body in each next moment and never in this very one. This young pup may grow into a wise, calculated, and embodied wolf if we ground ourselves in our present reality. With each mindful breath, we become the pack leader—a nurturing, commanding mother and a fearless, strong father.

Our wolf knows not of titles but instead embodies duality. They are not just the Divine Feminine or the Divine Masculine but are both and so much more. Our wolf leads in quiet strength, calmly navigates chaos, and commands presence without uttering a single word. We are cosmic beings, spiritual beings having a human experience. May we walk alongside our wolf, not only embodied but in-body.

Art is no less vital to me than the air I breathe or the water I drink. Thick paint courses through my veins with vibrant colors pumping through every heartbeat. Each inhale a symphony of rhythms. Each exhale a flow of poetry. Art is how I relate to the worlds—my inner world, the outer world, and the other world. Art is that bridge between, fluidly carrying me back, forth, and throughout. Art is the loom on which I can weave these worlds together in a vibrant, expansive tapestry. The material world confuses and confounds my artistic spirit, only finding sense in the metaphoric and metaphysical. The intention of my art is not only to express these visions but to find relation with those other souls who walk this same Earth. And as we relate to one another, I, too, hope to bridge relations to what is higher, what is most Divine, and what binds us all.

Kya Dubois
www.souloftheboreal.ca

DISCLAIMER

This book offers health and nutritional information and is designed for educational purposes only. You should not rely on this information as a substitute for, nor does it replace professional medical advice, diagnosis, or treatment. If you have any concerns or questions about your health, you should always consult with a physician or other healthcare professional. Do not disregard, avoid, or delay obtaining medical or health-related advice from your healthcare professional because of something you may have read here. The use of any information provided in this book is solely at your own risk.

Developments in medical research may impact the health, fitness, and nutritional advice that appears here. No assurances can be given that the information contained in this book will always include the most relevant findings or developments with respect to the particular material.

Having said all that, know that the experts here have shared their tools, practices, and knowledge with you with a sincere and generous intent to assist you on your health and wellness journey. Please contact them with any questions you may have about the techniques or information they provided. They will be happy to assist you further!

DEDICATION

The Universe provides teachers in all forms of life.

To the trees and bees, sand, and the sea.

Souls in fur form wild and free.

I love you and thank you

For the lessons far and wide.

Wanted or unwanted

We are here for the ride.

Our hearts reach to the cosmos

To help sing our tune

Communing with the elements,

Howling to the moon.

We give thanks

To the great Mother,

Her portal is divine

We are students of the Universe,

The Mystery School of infinite time.

Solar Hugs and Many Blessings to Life.

TABLE OF CONTENTS

CHAPTER 22

SERVICE THROUGH LEADERSHIP | 251

LEADING FROM THE HEART AS YOUR NEW WAY OF LIFE

By Angel and Seth Rohrer

INTRODUCTION

WAY OF THE WOLF

LEADERSHIP LEARNED FROM NATURE

Seth and Angel Rohrer

In our western culture, the idea of division comes in as the haves and the have-nots. It's not necessarily about the color of your skin or the birth status of an individual. We've chosen capitalism as our culture. And in the capitalist culture, it's the haves and the have-nots.

In this culture of haves and have-nots, leadership has been confused and intermingled with being above or better than, in some perceived way, by having more; more money, more power, more authority, and more status. At work you're perceived as a leader based on the status of your job title. We give our movie stars the status of being greater than others due to their high visibility and riches. In doing so, we give them a position of leadership. We give their words more weight, and we pay more attention to what they have to say. When they're actually just a person doing a job that gets paid more than most and is seen more than the rest of us, at their core, they're still as lost or traumatized as anybody else, if they haven't done their inner work. Leadership in western culture has been confused because of this.

Leadership has nothing to do with status, having more, rank, or job title. Leadership can be found in any human, at any level of the hierarchy system, and within any culture. You don't have to be born of royal blood or into a wealthy family to be a leader. True leadership is a way of being. A true leader does not have to use their position of power, higher rank, higher job title, or their status as having more riches and fame to inspire others to greatness. There is the key—inspire.

Leadership is the ability to inspire others by shining your light, owning your power which comes from within, and balancing the masculine and feminine energies that flow through each one of us. Leadership, as defined in Western culture, is imbalanced. It's a masculine-dominant (do as I said because I'm the boss or I'm a leader because I'm the boss and I'm in charge) dominance. That is not leadership. That's management; that is authority. Don't get me wrong, those are valid attributes in a workplace or organizational structure, but that does not equal leadership. Leadership isn't about getting people to do what you say.

Leadership is about showing people there's a more powerful and authentic way to live. Leadership is about growing people into a higher vibrational state of who they are. Leadership is about knowing people and connecting with their essence to allow you to foster their spirit, to foster that star seed within them waiting to be awakened, waiting to be summoned into action by them.

No one can make another person want or desire anything. When we say a leader inspires, we mean a leader calls forth and awakens that light. They awaken the creative genius that has lied dormant. Leadership brings inspiration from within another person, not by telling them how or what to do, but by inspiring their soul with your soul. There's an energetic connection that brings forth something in them that they didn't know was there and may not understand—joy, love, or creativity.

If you're looking for people to follow you, that doesn't make you a leader. A leader may be out in front at times, but this isn't because they're looking for people to follow them. They're out in front, because they're paving the path for others to cover the same ground with greater ease and to create a platform for those people to launch beyond what they've even believed possible of themselves. Leaders are way-showers.

Leadership is not management, task mastering, or getting people to toe the line of your organization and do what they're told. Leadership is about fostering that growth that will allow the spirit to come forth and be exactly what it is meant to be on this planet. Sometimes that looks like an inspired employee who does remarkable things for a company, and sometimes that looks like an inspired employee who leaves because they're miserable in what they do, and you have inspired them to follow their desires and support them in doing so.

Both are examples of beautiful leadership from the shamanic perspective.

WOLF MEDICINE

Wolf medicine embodies true authentic leadership and finding the path within. Native Americans and Celtic customs regard wolf medicine as the way to find the deepest levels of self, inner knowing, and intuition. They are the pathfinders and the way-showers of the planet Earth. Connected to the star Sirius, they carry ancient medicine for humanity. When we talk about animal medicine, we talk about the lessons we can learn from observing the way that animals show up in their world.

As we observe the wolf, we see and admire their wildness and fearlessness. In fact, most people fear those qualities that wolves mirror, as humans have been subjugated either by society or themselves and have no idea how to tap into that feral part of themselves. Society has programmed us to become civilized, yet we are still animals with wild spirits within.

To access our true authentic power and strength, humans can look to the wolf to inspire us to take risks, face our deepest fears, and learn to listen to our higher selves to show us the way through life and create the most beautiful dream right here on Earth. Wolves understand that there does not need to be hard separation between the solitary and social paths of life. Balance is key as you navigate family needs versus the needs within yourself. Wolves are fiercely loyal to their pack but do not give up their identity for the pack either.

There are times in your life when being a lone wolf in your own wilderness is needed. This is how you learn to access your channel, connect to the divine energy that is there for us all and gain trust in your own intuition. And wolves love to be social and thrive in a pack. They also mate for life; puppy love is a thing!

They are true masters when it comes to balancing community and solitude. With that mastery, the pack then becomes a powerful wave of transformation and change when it chooses to step into unfamiliar territory, set new intent for the pack, and become pathfinders of that area.

The alpha male chooses his mate and together they create their pack. When another wolf challenges for the position of alpha, and they show they can better serve the pack, the old alpha steps down to make way for the new alpha and shifts his position within the pack, knowing he's still loved and supported in his new role. The new alpha steps up to serve the pack to the best of his ability in protection, finding food, creating life, and growing the pack in strength and numbers together with his alpha female.

Wolf medicine provides lessons to humans on how to hold the divine feminine and divine masculine energy within us as individuals and how to show up and navigate aspects of our family or community. It understands every single soul that shows up in the community has an extremely vital role to play in way-showers. Each soul has been given a blueprint for their mission and those connected to their star family will receive information to bring to their pack. All wolves have medicine. All members of the pack share respect, gratitude, and wisdom with each other as they serve humanity's highest good.

This wolf medicine is present in each one of us. We define this as alpha and omega or masculine and feminine. The challenge for us on this planet is the balance of the masculine and the feminine within. This is not referring to the physical depiction of man and woman. These are the energies within each of us and between all of us.

The masculine energy that has dominated the culture of the west and the planet for hundreds of years has created the situation we see around us now. The lack of balance has created hostility, poverty, and pain. Masculine energy is about doing, doing, doing. Yet within this disconnect that has happened between polarities, the patriarchal ways have become toxic and are not serving humanity the best during these times.

The feminine energy is nurturing, creative, and compassionate. When you balance masculine and feminine, alpha and omega, and embody that wolf medicine, you create an environment within yourself and outside of yourself that supports the growth and highest vibration of all of life.

You're reading this book because you're looking for a new way to approach leadership. Look to the wolf as an example to embody. Really take in and put into practice the lessons of balancing the analytical doing and heartfelt knowing and support of divine love. The chapters you're about to read and the tools shared will help you step through the challenges and hurdles placed in your way by others and yourself, preventing you from stepping into this power of true leadership. Take these tools and make them part of your practice; and we mean practice, practice, practice.

Only then will you see your life change and your leadership grow and evolve.

All our love on your journey.

CHAPTER 1

THE SACRED DANCE

HONORING THE DIVINE MASCULINE AND FEMININE WITHIN

Angel Rohrer

My Story

"Come to my house for two weeks and see what you think."

WTF. I just met this human, I have spent four days at a retreat with him previously and now he wants me to go to a different country to visit for two whole weeks, during the lockdown? Am I crazy to say yes?

I started challenging myself when I asked myself if I was crazy by repeating the mantra given to me by one of my first shamanic mentors, "If you are sane enough to contemplate whether or not you are crazy, you aren't." Dropping in and listening to my body, the "yes" was authentic, and so began my next adventure, marked by my 50th birthday portal.

Two weeks turned into flowing with more "yes" as we did the sacred dance. I chose to lean into my omega feels, surrendering and allowing myself, for the first time in my life, to be consciously led by an alpha, a captain in the fire service.

The wiggles were real, forcing me to surrender to depths I had never swum in. His capacity to 'out-warrior' me was strong, which allowed my goddess to peek her head out and experiment with the mystery surrounding her while I felt safe and held in this space.

Soon into our courtship, an adventure called as the world attempted to navigate COVID and the restrictions put upon us humans. One warrior said "no" to the institution that was challenging his beliefs on vaccinations, and choices were made to leave his community and go where his values were accepted.

We said yes in support of this member of my alpha's pack and helped his family move from the West Coast all the way to the other side of the country via moving trucks.

The days turned to nights, and the sun came up and down as we drove across the country, state to state, entering different time zones, realities, and worlds. My consciousness expanded into the stars, sleeping, dreaming, driving, lulling me into lucidity as we covered 33 hours of road, stopping only to fuel and empty our truck and soul baskets.

Sleep came easy with the hum of the road, lulling me into dreamtime.

> *I was on my aunt and uncle's property in the mountains, visiting Uncle Jerry. Man, I have not seen him in forever. His eyes were as sparkly as the last time I saw him. Was it yesterday? My heart was exploding with joy as we walked the property, through the trees, smelling the fresh mountain air. He talks about connection with the land through his eyes, with no words escaping his half-shaven face. Memories flash of our most heartfelt moments in this lifetime, reminding me how special this soul was to me in its human form.*

Sunlight blinds me, searing into my eyelids, forcing my consciousness to wake into the here and now as the sun greets another day. As I sit up, feeling the vibration of the highway beneath my hip, I smile thinking: *What a great visit with Uncle Jerry. Wait a minute, he's been dead for 20 years.*

My body freezes as I come into full consciousness, looking around my unique environment, processing where I just was, looking down at my soul basket, reminding myself where I am, who I am with, and what we're doing. I softly run my hands down my arms, leaning into the cozy nest of furry blankets and sacred space created in the cab of the moving truck. A smile greets my face as I look out the window at the passing trees, "I am in my own mitote ceremony," I comment to myself as I take in the beauty of the rising sun.

We're helping this family to move across the country, honoring their decision to not vaccinate and relocate their eight children and two dogs to the East Coast. Members of the pack are starting a new life and storyline in a different part of the country. These are experiences to practice unconditional love and standing in my power and supporting humans where they're at.

The ocean called and this family answered. We are witnessing wolves stand in their power, honor their internal guidance, and follow their instinct to be of service in a different community. They are not backing down from those questioning and attempting to subjugate the husband within his career. We are holding space for his wife as she births her eighth child during the last full moon as they sell their family home and start packing for their new adventure, simultaneously welcoming a new baby girl into this world.

I am an outsider. Yet, I am in this truck, moving their life to South Carolina. Here, I have an opportunity to practice full goddess presence, resilience, and an open heart. There is an opportunity to stay expanded in the wife's presence of judgment and unacceptance, as I am 'the other woman.' I challenge her agreement that divorce is not okay, in her Christian belief system.

I witness my body during the discomfort, acknowledging and supporting myself in solo practice. Thankful for the tools provided, I recite mantras, do breathwork, and honor my body by removing myself when my energy is too low to maintain my nervous system as she slowly works through her own agreements.

We acknowledge the death cycle she is in. New baby, new home, a new state, new life, as she wrangles eight children in the middle of a pandemic as her alpha chooses to leave his job. I repeat the mantra: new baby, new home, new state, new life; as I practice not taking her distance personally. I am overwhelmed by the chaos of the moving trucks being unloaded by the three firefighters who drove across the country to help their brother and his family, part of their pack.

The beach calls to me, the sand between my toes, songs sung by passing birds, the sun sinking into and activating my cells as the waves softly roll into shore, alignment. This is sacred ground; tears fill my eyes as I scan the beach, "I could live here." I hear myself speak aloud, heart expanding, anchoring a container of energy, knowing deep within that I will return another day or lifetime to this beach. Or have I just returned?

The vibrations of the truck become a welcome initiation deep within myself, allowing and leaning into the stream of consciousness, recapitulating and rewriting storylines where I gave my own power away, sending healing to those timelines and releasing myself from those stories holding me back. I am dreaming, awake, following time with the movement of the sun. What day is it?

I feel expansion unlike ever before, embodying the present moment, forgetting there was even a moving truck in the parking lot at the Opryland Resort in Nashville on our one night of reprieve, in the process of moving a family.

Did we escape the matrix? I ask as we walk down hallways with no people in them. Stores are closed; restaurants are dark with no movement. There's creepy silence, and I joke about the fog outside looking like 'zombie weather.' *Are they hiding in here? Where is everyone? Is this simulator just for us at this moment?*

The carpet in the halls mesmerizes us into a hypnotic state every time we leave our room. I touch the walls as we walk, gazing into the sparkly lights on the ceiling. *Is this place real?* A noise pulls my attention, "Oh look! There is a human," he sings with the voice of an angel.

The soft, downy bed is a welcome change from the bench of the truck. Stretching out, I allow my soul-basket freedom and movement as I snuggle into the comfort and darkness of this new space. I find myself drifting off into a previous vision; it is so dark outside.

With the vision of the Eagle, I witness:

> This parking lot is expansive in the black of night. The huge building is blocking the wind as the family works to fix the bus-like RV parked against the brick building. There are tubes coming out of the bottom and sides. All are working tirelessly to fix the electrical system and restart the bus so they can carry on to their next destination.
>
> One by one, the tubes are untangled and cut until there is one left. Jose slowly walks the perimeter of the bus and joins the family inside.
>
> Time stands still as peace and reverence fill the air; stillness settles into space. The generations of the family quietly gather inside the bus, breathing in unison, merging with the infinite, as he is called home.

Waking up from my dream, moisture held in my eyes as my heart holds space for my loved ones. I turn on my computer and write...

Hearts

traversing in the infinite

Grazing past the stars and moon

Hearing calls from heaven

She called him home so soon

Honoring an

abandoned temple

Showering love

in a different tune

Grateful for this journey
Gratitude for you
Your love, your heart
your everything,
Inspires my heart's truth

Daring domestication
allowing our souls to thrive
We came to Earth
in avatars
Knowing the risk
to be alive

Our birthright
Our song
If the world could just get along
Peace and love
comes in all forms of size
I pray the world
one day
will come to realize

Blessings to you
for lighting the way
shining your bright light
As you whisper
words of wisdom...
I hear you in the night

The sun peeks into the room, into my eyes, gently bringing me back into the soft downy bed. I am filled with love and gratitude for this journey and space, and the humans who have chosen to join me in this storyline. Stepping into the parking lot of the Opryland Resort, greeting the full moon in all its glory, I take a moment to honor don Miguel Ruiz's brother, who crossed over the night before.

Breathe.

I am ready for the next part of this magical adventure I am on.

Feral and free, the full moon and me
Feral and free
the full moon and me
Sparkly lights
Shining down
shedding light
on the now

Presence is truth
the light shines so bright
My love
My heart
Beams gratitude for this night

Sea salt drips from my wet hair as we find our seats on the plane. I'm settling in and allowing the expansion room to play, drifting in and out, recapitulating what comes into my awareness, as the plane lulls me into lucidity.

Hours drift by, the sun long into slumber, our last plane to catch missed by minutes in the dark of night. My warrior within perks up: *The boys are on a 48-hour shift at 8 a.m. It's midnight, and we're in Seattle. Three and a half hours from home with no flights left tonight. Okay. I am driving. Scanning the airport, where's Starbucks? I need coffee.*

Don't make assumptions, I hear from deep within.

I pass along my thought process to my partner, who instantly rejects the offer. "Nah, I'm fine."

"But you both must work tomorrow, and I don't. You unpacked the entire truck by yourself today, then went surfing, then got on a plane that crossed the entire country!"

"This is what we do. We are doers."

Witnessing my jaw clenching and the fire building in my belly, I got still and checked in with my body:

Hey love, what's going on?

I am capable of leading.

I felt like I was not doing enough unloading the trucks

because I physically could not; this I can do.

I KNOW how tired they both are, driving that tired is a safety issue,

I will not sleep anyways

I have been expanded in goddess energy the whole trip,

my warrior is not being acknowledged at this moment.

Oh, he is forgetting we made an agreement to be agile with our aspects.

I need to use different language.

Thank you.

I turn to my partner and look deep into his eyes, "Hey Alpha, this is a perfect opportunity for you to practice being willing to receive."

An hour goes by as he stands alone in line getting the rental. As we head to the car, I inform the young cub I will be driving. The same dialogue shows up; the banter and giggles commence around their fast lifestyle and lack of sleep being normal in their world. This time, I just smiled and sent him so much love, knowing seeds will be planted tonight. I practice patience with the wolf cubs.

The little one chooses to drive first. He pops in the front seat, and I slide in the passenger seat, while my partner lays across the back with my furry blanket. At 1 a.m. I poke him, "Are you ready to switch?" He chooses the destination where we will switch, crawls in the back seat, and accepts the furry blanket offering.

An hour into my drive, the warrior beside me wakes, checks the GPS, and starts to talk. Interrupting him, "Aren't you supposed to be sleeping?" I grin, running my hand along the inside of his leg and up to his chest settling on his heart, "I got you." I energetically beam into his weary eyes, witnessing his body surrender and slide into a deep sleep.

I pulled into the driveway of the house left behind to drop off the warrior cub at his truck. Stirring, he exclaims, "Did you drive the rest of the way home? You brought me to my truck? Awesome!"

"I got you," escapes my lips, as he gathers his belongings and waves to my partner as he climbs into his vehicle. "See you in a couple of hours, Captain."

The alarm clock goes off after two hours of restful sleep in our own bed.

"Thank you for taking care of me." He whispers as he kisses my third eye and leaves to be in service to the citizens of our community, once again with his pack.

The start of a new day.

The Medicine

**Routines kill creativity. Yet, humans also need routines.
Where is the balance?**

When your routine is so hard wired, you slip into autopilot and miss a lot of what is going on around you. Your light, awareness, and sensitivities shut down.

The art of awareness demands creativity, attention, and intention.

**Can you undo some of your conscious patternings?
Or rather, are you *ready* to undo some of your conscious patternings?
You are wildly capable, and you always have a choice.**

Start with something little, like brushing your teeth with the opposite hand or taking a different route to get to work. How about ordering something different off the menu, or choosing a different type of music to listen to?

My big undoing experiment was to not drive when I came to Washington.

As a powerful, independent, single woman for years, being in control of my life was my normal. I chose to allow my partner to always be the one to drive, to be the consciousness, to be alpha, and lead. I chose not to memorize the roads and just be in the moment when we were in the vehicles, and completely surrender to the experience.

I had to train my body to sit with the discomfort of not being in control. I had to train my brain not to try to remember the roads or where anything was and just be in the moment.

This was a big ask for me, as a recovering controller. Control your environment, control your safety. Right? Does anyone else get nervous when someone else is driving?

I chose to stay in the experiment until I became comfortable with just being in the vehicle. Then, I started mapping the area and driving myself again.

Where can you be more present in your life and
SHED SOME LIGHT
onto some unhealthy patterns that are holding you back?

Six steps to release the snare around your paw:

1. Meet yourself where you are at.

2. Do not set yourself up for failure.

3. Choose attainable goals.

4. Assess and repeat.

5. Have fun with it!

6. Share your experience in the group.

Remember, the art of awareness demands creativity, attention, and intention.

Sharing your intention allows the Universe an opportunity to support you and your soul's growth in many magical and mysterious ways, yay!

**Mama Willow is so proud
of her wolf cubs and loves to post their
works of art on our den walls.
You deserve to be seen, you gorgeous ray of light!**

Angel Rohrer is a former high-performance coach in the power tumbling and trampoline world. She comes with 25 years of National-level experience training athletes of all ages and genders. After retiring, the last ten years were spent focusing her coaching skills in the holistic community, becoming a Crystal Reiki Master teacher and deep tissue massage specialist. She began coaching and healing those looking to wrangle their shadows of life as well as healing their physical body.

Ancient medicine has always been a calling. She spent 30 years mastering breathwork and moving energy through Kung Fu martial arts, as well as apprenticing with the Ruiz family (Author of *The Four Agreements*), Toltec Shamans of the Eagle Knight lineage, and honoring her own Celtic shamanic roots.

Join Angel and her husband Seth for journeys to the ancient city and pyramids of Teotihuacan, Mexico, the sacred sites of Peru, the Great Pyramids of Egypt, and more to be guided on your path to rediscovering the truth of who and what you are.

As Master Healers and shamans, Angel and Seth assist you in reclaiming your power, focusing your intent, and creating a life once thought impossible by most people.

As you walk your path through all that currently holds you back, you are not alone. Inner work does not mean lonely work. Angel invites you to join the Bytes of Light Den where you will find love, support, and assistance as part of a collective that celebrates your awakening to new gifts, applauds newfound awareness beyond the 3D, and encourages you to bring your fears into the light of our safe container.

Angel is also available for one-on-one work where the training will be specialized towards your highest growth, highest personal power, and truth.

Connect with Angel:

Website: https://www.rohrerrevolution.com

Facebook: https://www.facebook.com/bytesoflight

Instagram: https://www.instagram.com/angel.rohrer/

TikTok: https://www.tiktok.com/@angel.rohrer?lang=en

"Energetic agility is the secret sauce to keep authenticity alive in modernized gender roles."

~ Angel Rohrer

CHAPTER 2

ANCHORED IN TRUTH

ACCEPTING INTUITION AS YOUR GUIDE

Seth Rohrer

My Story

"Oh my God! You are having an emotional affair with this woman."

Why is she freaking out right now? How can she misread this situation like that? Why would she turn this into something sexual?

That's when it hit me like a brick wall. That is when I came to the realization of just how significant my experience had been. I cracked my Self open and quantum leaped into another state of being.

About a year and a half before this crack open, I stumbled across a podcast while attempting to increase my skills and knowledge in the realm of online business to create freedom in my life with online entrepreneurship. Who would've thought that business education would have been the catalyst to change my life?!

James Wedmore began integrating his esoteric and spiritual beliefs into the world of online business and entrepreneurship in a way my mind did not outrightly reject. It turns out that my life's situations and circumstances prepared me to receive his message in a way I never would've suspected.

The discovery of his podcast, Business by Design, led me to work with James as a business coach. This provided more galactic breadcrumbs. I discovered some of his mentors, which led to diving more deeply into the realms of mindset, ancient philosophy, and spirituality.

Along this path, I found a little book that kept popping up everywhere. It seemed like in every podcast I listened to on business or investment, the guests and hosts would consistently recommend this one little book, *The Four Agreements* by Don Miguel Ruiz. I read this book and it spoke to my soul. It resonated with truth. I felt it through my body. I began reading more of his books along with other similar books by other authors. I read and gobbled up all the information I was led to.

I began implementing the daily practices they suggested, and I began to see changes in my life.

I felt more peace inside, less chaos in my mind, more compassion, more understanding, and a deeper connection with the world around me. I liked it! I sought out more ways to learn from and work with Don Miguel Ruiz and found he offered retreats to a place called Teotihuacan, Mexico.

This was right during the middle of Covid during early fall 2020, so naturally nothing was available right away. The website said to check back frequently for updates, and I sure as shit did. I checked back every week for months in hopes they would finally announce the date of their next journey to Teotihuacan, and then, it finally happened. There was a date. May 27, 2021. I immediately booked my tickets, made my reservations, and it was set. I was ready to dive into the teachings and the community of Don Miguel Ruiz and the Toltec wisdom.

This was a trip I'd go on alone and a journey I needed to walk myself. My wife and I talked about the importance of adventuring together and adventuring alone, so it was no big shock when I explained to her that this felt like a journey I must walk by myself. She took my intention to fly solo well, and I encouraged her to seek her own opportunity for fun and adventure while I was gone. Or any other time she got the chance.

I went to Teotihuacan, with the intention of breaking out of my comfort zone, breaking out of that shell of not feeling comfortable approaching others and putting myself out there. That's why I needed to do it alone. I needed no safe place to hide and no security blanket. It had to be either approach people and make new friends or wallow in my own loneliness the whole five days. No easy outs. Sink or swim.

I set one other especially important intention for that trip: Be open to and follow my intuition to receive all the universe has for me in every moment.

I started introducing myself and putting myself out there before I even left the airport in Mexico City, and it went well. I was careful not to glom onto the first people I met as a new safety blanket, so I purposefully kept looking for new opportunities to meet new people. It was lunchtime on day three, and everyone was going their own way in small groups to find food outside of the hotel we stayed at. I felt that the right opportunity would show itself if I just milled around and waited. After everybody left the hotel to go eat, there it was. I milled myself around into eating lunch by myself.

That was not intuition after all. I just made that shit up in my head, and now I guess I will just eat lunch here by myself today. Oh well.

As I made my way toward the restaurant, a woman emerged from somewhere I didn't see, and she sat at one of the tables outside.

Oh shit! There's someone you have not met yet. Maybe I didn't make it up!

Okay. This is what you committed to. There she is, so go introduce yourself.

"Hello, I have not met you yet. My name is Seth."

She looked up from her book and our eyes met. For a moment she eyed me, not sure how she'd respond.

"I'm Angela, feel free to join me," as she set her book on the table.

Three hours later, we hardly stopped to take a breath. We discovered synchronicity after synchronicity after divine timing that brought us to that moment. Within the first 20 or 30 minutes of sitting down, we knew we were not meeting for the first time—just the first time in this life. There was a deep connection, and our souls had known each other for many lifetimes.

We knew we had work to do on this planet.

I told her how my wife and I were working to build an online business, how perfectly what she had to offer would tie in with our business, and how amazing I knew it would be. After a few more days of ceremony with the group and conversations in between activities, there was no question there was more for us to do. We shared an unconditional love that ran deep like a soul family, and I was excited to share this news with my wife.

On the last night of this magical retreat, we had a special surprise of authentic Aztec dancers and a ceremony. I do not know why or how, but this ceremony of the Aztec dancers and drumming impacted me in a way I could've never imagined. During that ceremony, my heart was cracked open, and my body convulsed all over—not so much that I fell to the ground, but it was no ordinary shiver either. My body had a physical, emotional, spiritual, and mental reaction to the drumming, dancing, and ritual involved, and it was amazing. It shifted my being in ways I wouldn't even know for weeks and months to follow.

The retreat ended and I returned home the next day. I knew I had an epic story to share with my wife, and I wanted to wait for the right moment to sit down with her and share how it all unfolded so beautifully from beginning to end. As I started sharing this epic story with her, I saw she was expecting something, and wasn't reacting the way I expected. Before I finished telling my story, she blurted out that line that changed our lives forever.

"You need to cut off all communication with that woman and never speak to her again, and you will spend the rest of our lives earning back my trust!"

Wham! There it was. The gauntlet dropped, and I was faced with a choice. Never associate with or talk to this person who I'd made a soul connection with and submit myself to a life of walking on eggshells in hopes that one day my wife might trust me again after a crime I didn't believe I committed or stand my ground in this truth and highly likely end a relationship of seven years.

The part most shocking to me as these events unfolded and her emotions began to spiral out of control, was that I remained calm and at peace within myself. This was new even for me. I've always been mellow, but this was off the charts. My marriage was potentially falling apart, and there I sat, grounded and at peace with whatever the outcome may be.

This reaction, or lack thereof, was interpreted by my wife as not caring and callous, but it was the opposite. My love and compassion were so deep for myself and for her that I couldn't be shaken. It may sound crazy to some people, and I get that. A few weeks before, I, too, would've thought this impossible, but I accessed a deep truth within—the truth of what I am: Divine love.

Even faced with the potential end of our marriage, I was resistant to cutting ties and communication with Angela, because my heart and soul knew she'd be a significant part of my divine purpose on this planet, but I also did not wish to end my marriage. This concept was not on my radar.

What I wasn't prepared for was the quantum leap I took from who I was when I left, to who I was when I came home. I learned in time that the human who left for Teotihuacan never came home. That human died a spiritual death in the belly of Quetzalcoatl and walked the avenue of the dead to be reborn from the temple of the moon, but that is a whole other story I'd love to share with you another day.

After a month of attempting to find common ground to move forward, it was made clear to me that my wife wouldn't accept my new way of being.

"Is this all because this is a woman that I had this experience with?"

"No!"

"So, you're telling me, if this had been a man that I had this connection with and wanted to bring into our business because he had such great tools to offer and we had this soul connection as if he was my brother and I loved him, that you would still be this upset."

"Yes, I would. I do not want you to give your love away to other people. I want your love to be just for me."

At that moment I knew there was no moving forward. My heart opened and I received the message loud and clear. This divine love I rediscovered was to be shared with the world. I could choose where I wanted to lay my affections and how I wanted to share my intimacy, but my love was for everyone who was ready and open to receive it.

The Medicine

As we create our story and walk the path that unfolds before us, we're going to encounter opportunities for great, expansive growth. When these moments come, they can be shocking and unnerving. You may even feel the fight, flight, or freeze of your fear response ramp up in your brain.

When we step out of our everyday lives to explore the truth of who we are; when we go to these amazing places and meet amazing people who are also working to open their hearts, we're lifted to new levels of awareness and to new vibrations we never could have imagined before. As we go back to the world we created from our previous level of consciousness and vibration, it can feel like stepping into a foreign land.

It's in these moments we must make a choice. Am I going to be true to my heart and transform my life to reflect my new empowered and loving self, or am I going to attempt to subjugate myself by stuffing myself back into a life that no longer fits?

You might be asking yourself; how do I know the difference between what will serve me at that point and what will not?

You walk around all day, every day, with the greatest lie detector that has ever existed—your guts! Own your guts. Know your guts. They are of service to you in many ways.

First, we must address the discomfort that can come from the unknown and change in your life. The brain has one function, to keep the soul basket alive. It's quite effective at carrying out this directive. It keeps thousands of functions going on in your body at any given time without a single conscious thought from you.

It also likes predictability. If it has seen or experienced it before, it knows how to calculate a result, regardless of whether the situation or circumstance is elevating your life or creating trauma. This's why people stay in abusive relationships, and why the cycle of abuse continues through generations.

You cannot rely on your brain to make decisions in areas of personal evolution and transformation. It does not like change.

However, your heart knows the way if you'll choose to listen. Your heart will tell you whether it's truth or fear driving your actions and thoughts.

Can I go back to who I was?
Can I be the version of me that I was before?

We have all felt that tightness in the chest, that uncomfortable feeling in our stomach, or that fight-or-flight when there is no real physical danger. This is fear. Decisions made from fear create a life based on lies, or a miscreation of life.

The other side of that coin is the feeling of peace, joy, calm, and love. When we're holding this inner state of being, we're in our truth and alignment with our divine purpose. We're in alignment with life itself.

When faced with a big decision, take time to remove yourself from outside distractions to address each option individually. Find a quiet comfortable place and ground into your body with some long deep breaths all the way down into your pelvis. Do this until you are feeling calm and at ease, and then ask the question:

Should I walk this path?

Notice your body's reactions. Move your attention to your heart space, stomach, back, neck, or other parts of your body that might be sending you a message. There are three ways to determine the choice that'll serve your highest good. Remember to ask about one option at a time.

One, you notice a heartwarming and peaceful feeling, and your whole body is at ease. This is a slam dunk clear message that this option is in alignment with your divine path.

Two, you find your stomach doing summersaults with a feeling of nausea or disgust or just a general feeling of discomfort. This is a clear no.

Three, you feel your fight-or-flight ramping up. Your chest gets tight, and your pulse quickens. Fear is rearing its head. This can feel confusing, scary, or both, but it's a clear answer either way. This fear is the mind's attempt to keep you from stepping out of your comfort zone. However, if you want to experience life beyond your wildest imagination, this is a yes!

Whether it be peaceful or scary, listening to your body and following the yes will lead to a path of alignment with your divine purpose, your most beautiful expression of life, and creating your Heaven on Earth.

As you practice this presence and grounding exercise for making big choices, you may even begin to receive audible or visual signs for yes or no.

Peace, joy, and fear can tell you which decision serves you best once you learn how to listen to them.

The heart knows the way home to truth and back to connection with your higher self and divine love, so while you are doing the work to let go of your fears, know that those fears are also your guide and teacher.

**If you have the courage and the commitment to yourself
to be afraid and do it anyway, you'll create magic.**

You will discover joy and love and you'll author a beautiful story of Heaven, such as you cannot even imagine at this moment.

Own your guts. They will guide you. You must learn how to listen.

All my love and all my gratitude for receiving these words.

Seth has spent countless hours in his pursuit of love, service, and wisdom. His spiritual journey is one of heart. His mission is to help people shift their awareness and level of consciousness, so they can transform their lives and step into their unique gifts and cosmic power. His nearly 20 years in the fire service in various leadership, mentorship, and instructional roles gives him a unique perspective and ability to guide you through intense inner work to discover, accept, and shine the light on the shadows and heavy energy in your body to reclaim your power and create a beautiful story of Heaven during your time here on Earth.

Join Seth and his wife Angel for a journey to the ancient city of Teotihuacán, Mexico, the magnificent sites of the Sacred Valley and Cusco in Peru, the Great Pyramids of Egypt, and more to be guided on your path to rediscovering the truth of who and what you are. As Master Healers and practicing shamans, Seth and Angel assist you in reclaiming your power, focusing your intent, and creating a life and inner state of being once thought impossible by most people.

As you walk your path through all that currently holds you back, you are not alone. Inner work does not mean lonely work. Seth invites you to join the Bytes of Light Den, where you will find love, support, and assistance as part of a collective that celebrates your awakening to new gifts, applauds newfound awareness beyond the 3D, and encourages you to bring your fears into the light of our safe container.

If you are ready for more focused one-on-one work, Seth would be happy to assist you in rediscovering your inner power and your personal truth.

Join Seth on social media and check out his website to see how he can be of higher service to you in further creating your beautiful story of life.

Connect with Seth:

Instagram: Instagram.com/bytesoflight

Facebook: facebook.com/bytesoflight

Website: rohrerrevolution.com

"You walk around all day, every day with the greatest lie detector that has ever existed. Your guts! Own your guts. Know your guts."

~ Seth Rohrer

CHAPTER 3

YOUR LIGHT IS YOUR STRENGTH

CHILDREN OF THE SUN
EMBODY LEADERSHIP,
BEGINNING AND ENDING WITH LOVE

Jorge Luis Delgado

My Story

In the Andean tradition, we learn the most important messages from legends and stories that our grandfathers told us about the different experiences of life.

**Examples that inspire us humans to take initiative.
How we can arrive at diverse levels of awareness.**

One of these beautiful legends talks about a searcher who was in many ways successful in various aspects of life. He was successful with his career, nice family, good car, and house. It seemed that he was successful, but he knew something was missing. He was empty inside, so he decided to explore what would complete him and how he could experience his real self on a different level.

Success only in the material world is not all we're searching for.

He tried many ways and many modalities to try to fill that emptiness. He looked to politics and religions and many kinds of movements and groups of people.

Suddenly he got some news about people living in the mountains with a unique way of life. They are very connected with Mother Earth and the Father Sun.

Every experience is good, and part of our life learning, and everything we learn is getting us prepared to be the leaders of the new cycle.

He got all that experience and went to this community in the highlands. He found that there were many elders and wise people up there, so he decided to look for the oldest one. He thought that the oldest elder should have the deepest level of consciousness about awareness and how to find the real self.

When he arrived at this elder's house, he asked, "Grandfather, could you tell me what it is you can teach me?"

He said, "Yes. What is it that you want to learn?"

"I want to learn about my love." He had to start at some point, and he thought that after all his experiences, it was all about love.

The elder says, "Well, if you want to expand your love, the only thing you must do is share your love. No matter what, just share your love."

The searcher responds, "This is too simple. Maybe you can teach me a little bit deeper. I have the time and the money because I'm taking all this year for myself. I want to go deeper than this."

The elder says, "You know, it's quite simple. You must experience sharing your love with all your relations. With your mother, father, family, neighbors, your past, your future, and yourself."

"Okay. Then I can do it by myself?"

"Yes. You must do it by yourself. Nobody else is going to do it for you. Only you can do that."

When he returned home, he was extremely helpful to everybody. The family, the neighbors, and everybody that needed help. He would be the first one there.

He felt good assisting people and helping people, but at some point, he was still feeling that emptiness. He decided to return to the community in the highlands to talk to the elder.

He said, "Grandfather, could you tell me what I'm doing wrong here, I can really feel that feeling of good actions, but I'm still feeling that emptiness inside. What am I doing wrong?"

The elder said, "Okay. Let's see. How much more do you love yourself since the last time you were here?"

"Wait a moment. You never told me to love myself. You said to share your love with others."

"Yes, but if you do not know the frequency of that energy. If you do not experience love for yourself, how do you know what you're sharing is love? How do you know what you're sharing is light? Remember that light is always wise like love is always in service."

"Oh. That is a key point. I must learn how to love myself deeper."

"Yes. You got it."

He returned home and was learning deeper modalities to love himself. He found that being in gratitude is a way of love. To be grateful for all parts of his body, with life, and the relations. Everything was amazing for him just by being grateful.

His mind was watching and saying, *you got it. You are in a higher level of consciousness of love.*

He was excited and went to the elder again to confirm that he was already on the higher level of consciousness of love. Love is 'munay', and 'tucuy munay niyoc' is a higher level of consciousness of love. When he was asking if he was already at tucuy munay niyoc, the elder immediately said, "You are not there yet, my friend."

He was disappointed and returned home. After a while, he explored all the ways to love himself because he wanted to get to this higher level of consciousness of love. He experienced much coming from the heart, but one of the most amazing experiences was loving children. To love the inner child.

He thought that was it. When he arrived at the elder again, he asked, "Am I at tucuy munay niyoc?"

"You are not there yet."

He then learned a way to use warm words with himself. Positive words and thoughts. He went back to the elder and said, "Now I can warmly talk with myself, with much affection. Soft, and I always talk the truth to myself, because I can speak from my heart."

"You are doing very well, but you are not there yet."

"Really?!"

"Yes."

He returned home trying to find other ways.

This time when he returned to the home of the elder, the elder could see him coming from a distance and called out to him, "Hey my friend. You are not there yet."

"What? What do you mean? I did not even tell you what kind of experiences I've been having."

"Well, all that is not important, because it's just your mind. You're just in the mind that wants approval. Your mind wants a certificate that you're doing it and are in the higher level of love."

The truth is, it's the cosmos that tells you, you are there. You just feel it.

You just open all the doors, and you understand all this part of the experience. Then the cosmos sends you a messenger. In this case, it's a hummingbird that flies above your head trying to get the nectar from you, because you opened the resistance naturally without the mind.

When all your discernment is in your heart, then you're open to sharing your sweetness, affection, nectar, beauty, light, and life.

That means you understand life as one, you are wise, and you are love, but you must try it first as the hummingbird does without destroying the flower. Each of us, as we grow, need to have strong roots with Mother

Earth, and a strong connection with Father Sun, so we can bloom any place and anywhere.

I wish you many hummingbirds in your life.

In this new day in this new world, it's so important to know everyone is in an evolutionary process.

In this process, we can see clearly that the process has to do with all our relations. In whatever we do in this lifetime, we impact our surroundings internally and externally. We are all interconnected; we are all interdependent as we are one community of children of the light. We have this great opportunity to bring our strength from our inner sun from our real self to bring the evolution for the expansion of consciousness.

In my beloved country of Peru, recently, people have been arguing about the idea of having a new constitution for our country. Some people believe that the transformation will happen through love. Some people believe a new constitution will bring happiness, freedom, or joy. But within each of us, we know that only in the pathway of the evolution of our consciousness lays the opening of the endless spring of love; service and wisdom from our hearts is the only way.

But as much awareness we bring about the meaning of that light, we can see that the leaders of the evolving world must be leaders that love themselves. There are no new leaders that do not love themselves. Because if you do not love yourself, you do not love Mother Earth, and you do not love your relations. It's important to accept your inner wisdom.

Listening to our hearts harmonizes our relations.
Everybody will make an important contribution to the evolution
of life.

Releasing resistance, releasing the blockages that do not let us be who we are, is our first mission. We have the ability; we have the gifts to transform. We use the qualities of the light that Father Sun is teaching us every day: clarifying our past, creating transparency in our lives, and accepting the luminosity of our luminous bodies. Accepting the gifts and talents we bring, we can share the brightness of our souls and the brightness of our hearts. Of course, together with our bright minds.

**New leadership starts by loving ourselves.
The new leadership continues by sharing that love.**

Sharing our love makes us and our gifts stronger and stronger. Diving into the mysteries of life, surrendering, and discovering new rays of light in this new world will give you opportunities to grow and expand and find new gifts you didn't know you had. Perhaps you don't know exactly what the biggest gift is we receive from Mother Earth, life, the cosmos, and our relations. For sure, we will realize the most important gift we can give to ourselves is to feed our soul and nurture our souls to let the light of the mother and the father come through our experiences of life.

Many of us on this planet and across the world have been planting seeds of knowledge for this new society, dreaming into the new world, and planning to build new communities connected in light. All the seeds exist for humanity; it's now possible for all of humanity to bloom. Within this blooming, there also is a deep need for rooting in. It's essential to have deep roots to make our relationship stronger with Mother Earth.

Mother Earth is calling for humanity to help open the resistance to the light. Open to the love, service, and wisdom of Father Sun.

Every day Father Sun shares with us. As much as we consciously choose to connect with that light, we embody that light, we become more aware that light is love. We are aware that no light is not wise.

The light is always wise, so we always choose light.

We always know that light is in service to the light. The new evolutionary success in leadership focuses on our natural, authentic ability to bring our contribution to life on this planet. In this life, everything is reciprocal. Reciprocity happens in our lives from different directions; it's multi-dimensional. And it's happening right now as we connect with this valuable tool. Heart-centered awareness, living from your intuition, and being in a consistent space of being in service will reflect that unique ray of light to you in your own life.

We have the most important strength, our power, which is light.

For our ancestors, the Incas, light is power—the power that stays forever. Anchoring the new light for the new world is building foundations for the new society and the new paradigms that have to do with the most important meaning of life, the new pachacuti.

**The return to the sun, the return to light,
the return to sacredness, the return to the divine.**

It's from the divine self we can harmonize ourselves and our duality. We can harmonize life. It starts with the love that we open to ourselves.

The society of love is the society of wisdom reflected in the way we experience life, and naturally, we are harmonizing all our relations.

The Medicine

To feed and nourish our soul and allow ourselves to bloom we must connect to the sun and embody its light. Ceremonies and practices may support your evolution by helping you step into your birthright as a Child of the Sun.

Before doing any ceremony, it's important to review and set your intent. This is especially true when we're releasing the debilitating energy of Hucha (dark energies).

Intent plays with the world of possibilities, and with the Divine Mother, everything is possible.

No matter what has happened or how much we're suffering, the intent in our hearts will always be connected to the Universe. It's vital for us to enter into these powerful, healing ceremonies with a pure, clear purpose. We must demonstrate our conviction and commitment to self-healing by doing these ceremonies wholeheartedly.

The most important thing is to go into the ceremony with an open heart and participate using the purest part of yourself, and requesting permission from Mother Earth and the spirits that reside in that sacred space.

Understanding the differences between intent and intention is also important during the ceremony. Intent comes from your heart and is connected to your life force energy which all your visions and possibilities are birthed from. Intention comes from your brain and is based on expectations and rationalizations.

To release the Hucha within takes the heart life force of your intent.

GREETINGS OF THE SUN PRACTICE

We, as descendants of the Inka, have many ways of liberating ourselves from Hucha and overcoming heavy energies. In this greeting of the sun practice, we gain energy as we surrender our darkness over to the light and connect our own cosmic energy to Father Sun and Mother Earth in an encounter of high intensity.

1. Find a place where you can see Father Sun in the east. Lift your head to the sun and invite the light into your cells with your arms outstretched as you breathe deep within your lungs. Eyes can be open or closed as you show gratitude for this moment.

2. Allow your arms to fall to your side as you allow yourself to merge with the rays of light. Reach to the light with your right hand and either in your head or aloud say the words "in love" as you grasp the filaments of the light in your hand and bring them to your heart and hold the nourishing energy in your chest.

3. With your left hand, reach to the light and either in your head or aloud, say the words "without fear" as you grasp the filaments of the light in your hand and bring them to your sacral area, holding the light to transmute any dark energies residing within. As you feel it bubble up, pull it out with your left hand, away from your body, and direct it toward Mother Earth to transmute into pure light.

4. Repeat as many times as needed to feel your clear channel open and flowing. Allow yourself to be nourished by this light and as it starts to overflow, extend that love to humanity. The power, from where we share the love we have within, comes from this clear place.

5. The deeper you surrender, the more you experience the light. Keep your intent in the forefront of your heart as you connect your own inner sun to the light of Father Sun.

6. Connection to the sun is key to not only the energy but to the humans, plants, and animals surrounding you. Look to a person, plant, or animal and share your light with them as they reflect you, your unique ray of light, and allow that energy flow to surge through you.

7. You will remember, in this heightened state of awareness, you are one with all there is.

Gratitude, love, service, and wisdom are medicine.

Jorge Luis Delgado was born in the Andes mountains of Peru.

He is a descendant of Quechua and Aymara native cultures. A lover of ancient wisdom, Jorge Luis became a "chakaruna" (bridge person) at the age of 11 and began to assist and show Pilgrims and travelers how to find their way.

He shares his solar heritage all over the world including North, Central, and South America, Europe, and Asia. As a founding member of the Brotherhood of the Solar Disk society, he is a way-shower for this 10th Pachakuti in this world that is now being turned upside down.

He is known and respected by the Andean Priests, Priestesses, and the Indigenous people of the region and has been highlighted on the TV show *Ancient Aliens* in over ten episodes.

As a great organizer of world events, and an activator of portals and the expansion of consciousness, Jorge teaches that a new consciousness is emerging, one leading to a golden age that was activated in 2012.

He is the owner and founder of Kontiki Tour Company and owns hotels in Cusco, the sacred valley, Aguas Calientes (Machu Picchu), and on the shores of Lake Titicaca.

He is a keeper of ancient knowledge and uses it to assist in healing for all who are ready.

To go on one of his sacred power journeys or to connect further with Jorge see below.

Website: kontikiperu.com

Email: Kontiki@kontikiperu.com

Facebook: jorgeluis.delgado.311

Instagram: jorgeluischakaruna

*"We have the most important strength, our power, which is light.
The light is always wise, so we always choose light."*

~ Jorge Luis Delgado

CHAPTER 4

MEDICINE WALK
A PATH OF DIRECT REVELATION

Atlantis Wolf

Why bother connecting to spiritual realms? You could save your life. I saved mine.

Shamanism is ritualized animism, the ancient belief that everything we can see and touch is animated with a soul, a spiritual component married to a physical form. A shaman practices connecting to that unseen terrain, normally with their eyes covered or closed, using ceremonies aligned with the spirals of planetary cycles and human rites of passage. The word shaman means 'one who sees in the dark.'

Shamanism is a spiritual practice based on direct revelation. You are your own shaman. There is no guru, priest, or rabbi leading the way. Your personal experience in shamanic journeys and rituals gives you the answers you need if you are practicing with integrity. Detach your ego from the outcome and ask spirit guides for help. Ask from a place of love, not fear. Spirit guides do not have physical bodies. They might come to you in your mind's eye in the form of animals, ancestors, or angels. Or even dragons.

My Story

"Bruce, I'm running off to work!" I shouted up the stairs from the kitchen as I pulled on my second boot and snapped my purple coat off its hook.

"Okay, Mom, see you soon," he replied from behind his closed bedroom door.

One of my black cats, Pontos, sat his meatball-sized body next to his empty food bowl and turned his bear cub cheeks and green eyes at me as I shoved my cell phone into my purse, slung my bag with massage sheets over my shoulder, and grabbed my lunch from the fridge.

Dammit, I thought.

"Bruce, can you feed the cats their tuna fish?" I shouted. "And scoop the litter? I don't have time."

"Yep," he answered.

I hurried to the garage, snatching the mail from the mailbox. As I walked and shuffled through the mail, I saw a letter with the return address of the City of Amherst, New York.

Dammit to hell, I thought as I dumped it and my bags on the passenger seat and started my car.

I forgot to call in for the speeding ticket I got over the holiday break in Buffalo. First one in years. Years! I missed my chance to get the fine reduced.

I called my friend, John, who I always call on my way to work.

"Hiya!" I said.

"Good morning!" he replied, "How are you, Sunshine?"

"Pretty good, rushing off to work. I'm free this Thursday if you want to go out to dinner at L'Albatros or somewhere close."

He said, smiling, "I feel like you're always rushing to work. Thursday is great. Let's talk Wednesday. I have to take this call."

I drove past my favorite nature reserve and saw a hawk perched on a high branch.

It must be nice to be just sitting there, I thought. *No time to ask for a message today, my friend. I'm running late, maybe on my way home.*

I careened through the familiar bends and curves past the green parklands and blue lake into my last right turn. One residential city block away from work. Last lap in the home stretch.

Ha! I thought. *I'm totally going to make it. I've got four minutes!*

I slowed to a pause as I came up to my stop sign, looking right at Roxboro school's soccer field bounded by the long stretch of chain link fence. I swiveled my head left—empty street. Back to the right quick as a bird. Oversized white Ford pickup truck to my right, pulling into the driveway of the stone century house on the corner.

Yes! I thought. *All good.*

I accelerated, zipping over the cross-street. Halfway across in the middle of the road, a curved flash of tan appeared to my right, outside my passenger door. It was so close I couldn't even see the bumper. But I saw the logo on the hood—Nissan.

Oh no! I thought, sucking in all my breath.

Time switched to slo-mo video mode.

The black bumper crashed into my red Volkswagen at the crossbar between the front and back doors, shattering the glass windows. The impact on the metal body came with a sound of an elephant's groan and a rippling wave of energy that tossed my head and neck first to the right then left into my driver's side window with a stone-like crack. The front passenger tire was pushed inward, straining at the axle, as the back end of the car was beginning to spiral into oncoming traffic.

The moment unfolded around me as if I was sitting at the center of a white thousand-petal lotus, opening petal by petal. I thought, *Double-damnit! I'll have to get the car fixed. If it can be fixed. Am I hurt? Feel fine. Kinda wavy. What if I have to stop working again? Rent. Mortgage. I'll have to tell my dad. I'll be late for work. I don't have time for this. Oh! This might be bad. Super bad. My head is going to hit the window again. That's going to hurt. This might be worse than I can imagine. Lights out? The end?*

I closed my eyes, letting go of the choking tension circling around my body like a claw, and whispered, "No."

Darkness swallowed me. A moment of black silence, nothingness. Stillness.

I arrived in the driver's seat of my car parked in front of the stone house on the corner. My body was uninjured and my car undamaged. I looked around. *All good,* I thought. I looked through my window to the left and saw the tan Nissan sedan. He had stopped, back brake lights on. He saw me looking at him and then drove away.

What happened? I thought. I felt my body as if I had long antennae that were checking all of my skin. *All good.* My heartbeat was even and calm. There was no adrenaline pumping into my bloodstream. I couldn't have been more steady. My brain and body felt slow, like waking from a long afternoon nap in an empty house.

The car phased through your car, I heard my angel voice say in my head.

Oh, okay, I thought. *Sure. Like that story Grace told about her Chicago business trip. Okay. Okay. I'm okay. Okay, I'm going to work now. Do I work?*

I eased my foot off the brake and began to drive down the long tree-lined block with turn-of-the-century duplexes and three-story apartment buildings. It was sunny with a few clouds—a cool late-winter morning.

I heard two voices in my head, a child and an adult.

The adult's voice was saying things like: *How could that happen? Maybe it didn't happen. You could have been killed! You should be ashamed of yourself for not seeing that car. You're lucky to be alive. Don't tell anybody! What would Bruce think? Or your dad? He's paying for that car, you know.*

The child's voice was saying things like: *Wow! That was amazing! That might be the coolest thing that ever happens to me in my life. Man! Can't wait to tell Karla. This is out there even for me! I love how the sun comes through those tree branches. It'll be nice when the leaves come back. I'm so lucky this is my commute. I love seeing this neighborhood every day. Oh, now that's a pretty dog. What a floofy tail!*

I found a parking spot close to the back door and came to a stop. Two minutes early.

Amazing! I thought.

As I walked up the stairs, the adult voice started to get louder. *You're late. It's not professional. The client will be angry.* I stumbled at the last step, slowing down to open the landing door. My client was waiting on a chair in the hallway.

"Hi, Fred!" I said. "Sorry, I'm late."

Fred looked at his watch and said, "Looks like you're right on time."

We walked into my office and I turned on the Turkish lamp and pedestal knight lamp in the reception room, then the salt lamp and fairy lights in the center room. I set my bags in my Zoom room before heading to the massage room.

"Your room is ready," I said to him. "You can head in. I'll give you a second and knock before I come in."

He walked into the massage room, closing the door behind him. I walked back into my Zoom room and hung up my coat and purse, taking off my boots and slipping into my red wool slippers with a felt black cat across the top of them.

I picked up my black hematite dragon figure and closed my eyes, holding it against my chest. In my mind's eye my black guardian dragon with blue kyanite eyes appeared, surrounding me with his massive, warm, scaly body.

What was all that? I asked him.

Schism, he answered.

Oh, I replied. *I'm okay?*

You made a choice, he said.

I inhaled a short breath and exhaled an elongated sigh, grinning at my galactic dragon and his wide smile filled with 10,000 teeth. I opened my eyes and placed the figure back on the shelf.

I walked toward the massage room door. I knocked, turning the doorknob.

"All good?" I asked with a smile as I stepped inside.

The Medicine

The longer version of my story is that I was getting intuitive messages about getting into a car accident for months. I ignored them. I thought it was residual, ancestral energy I was healing. My grandmother was in a car accident in her 20s and never drove again. Both ideas could be true.

I believe my moment of clarity, my choice point, was possible because of my connection to Spirit—also because of my autism. My whirling brain is quick to analyze and assess. My connection to the spiritual world is a constant practice, as automatic as breathing. I shift between the physical and non-physical world every day as part of my work with massage and coaching clients. It's part of my human experience. I think of myself as a ferryman, taking people into the mist and back again. I share what I see and hear, then teach my clients how to do it.

My baseline practice is waking up and walking from my house into the woods. Everyday. In all weather (except sleet). Connecting to nature helps me feel part of the natural world, not separated from it. Forest bathing helps me find my pace when I'm unchained from deadlines, schedules, or knowing the day of the week.

I live in a historic, city suburb on Lake Erie. Developed in the 1920s, it has three lakes surrounded by forest. If you look in your community, you may be surprised to find a patch of forest or natural environs close to your home, too. Find somewhere you can be surrounded by trees, water, or rock formations.

'Medicine walk' is the phrase used by the shamanic community to mean a walking ceremony or to walk with the intention of asking Mother Nature a question. You can think of it as opening yourself to guidance while immersing yourself in a natural setting. There is no set amount of time required. Take as long as you need. I usually walk for 60 to 90 minutes.

You can follow my guidelines, or come with me on a walk in this YouTube video. https://youtu.be/1TMbD0coJsQ

ACCOMMODATIONS:

You might be thinking: *But, Atlantis, I can't walk for an hour. I can't even walk for five minutes! I don't live close to a forest or ocean. I'm too busy. I'm too old. I'm scared. It won't work for me.*

Start where you are. Set your own pace. Make accommodations for yourself. Meet yourself where you are today. Go out your front door and walk for a few minutes, then turn around and walk back. Walk four minutes today and five minutes tomorrow. A single tree works as well as a forest. A brook can guide you as well as an ocean. Your body will respond each time you practice even if you are only walking in your imagination.

WHAT TO BRING:

1. Layers of clothing to be comfortable as you get your inner fire going.

2. Small water bottle.

3. Dried fruit in case you walk longer than you intended and need a light snack.

4. Comfortable, closed-toed shoes. Walk with authority and keep your toes safe for walking on stones, dirt, mud, and puddles.

WHAT NOT TO BRING:

1. A cell phone. We are socially conditioned to be available 24/7. For some people it's a habit; for others an addiction. Unplug—phone off, heart open. If you need help, your spirit guides will send someone with a phone to help. You don't need it. You're just conditioned to have it. Free yourself for one hour a day.

2. Anything related to a cell phone such as an Apple watch, Fitbit, or heart rate monitor. If it beeps or burps, leave it at home.

3. A dog. This is not about multi-tasking. This is the time for you to open yourself to inner wisdom. Walk your wolf before or after.

4. A buddy. This is a solo adventure, a spiritual practice. This hour is for you to discover your own interior landscape reflected in the outer

world. This is not about your partner pointing things out for you. It's all about you, Love.

INTENTION SETTING

A ceremony is setting an intention and performing an intuitive ritual. Set your intention and choose your ritual. For example, I like to set the intention, 'Show me what I need to see today.' And as a ritual, I like to have my walking clothes hanging over the towel rack in the bathroom the night before so I can put them on without a thought. I like to put my socks in my shoes downstairs for the same reason. In the morning, I squeeze a lemon wedge into a glass and add water to start my daily digestion. I save coffee as my cup of celebration when I return from my triumphant walk. Another success!

SAMPLE INTENTIONS

- Observe your breath and how it changes over the walk.

- Look at patterns in tree trunks.

- How many animals do you see?

- Listen to your heartbeat.

SAMPLE RITUALS

- Set out your favorite fruit and cut it silently when you return, easing back to home life. Imagine where it came from, how it grew, and how it got to you.

- Step outside and breathe three times, in through your nose and out through your mouth as long as you can on the exhale. Then begin walking.

- Before you walk back into your house, greet your house with love and gratitude. Say, "Thank you for being my house (or apartment or room)."

- Make coffee or tea in silence, thanking everyone who had to work to provide you with the cup of coffee or tea in your hand.

THE WALK

As you walk, become the observer. Move from thinking to feeling, from your mind into your body. Give yourself permission to treat what is happening as a movie. Watch the movie. Begin to notice how each of your senses are reacting.

- Do you see birds, trash on the sidewalk, or details in the houses close to you?
- Do you feel the wind on your skin, the sun, or the humid air?
- How do your feet feel as they walk? Do you walk heel-to-toe or midfoot-to-toe? Does one leg feel longer than the other? Do you walk fast, slow, or somewhere in between? How do your hips feel?

Keep walking. Keep noticing. What is hooking your attention? What do you see or feel today? Do you see animal footprints or scat? Do you see birds in the sky? Do you notice which trees hold a bigger space than others?

AFTER THE WALK

Resist the urge to grab your phone. Breathe in your home space. Notice how it feels today. Observe the way the light fills your kitchen. Come back to your home routines with grace and a slowed pace. Remember what you observed in your walk and write it in a journal. Sit with your coffee or tea and journal into each of your senses, including emotions. Commit to journaling for ten minutes each day immediately after your walk. Then once a week, go back and read what you wrote.

As an experiment, write one word that describes your mood before you walk and one word after. Then play with other ideas, like focusing on one sense each day or looking at how sunlight illuminates things on the ground versus things in bushes or trees. Notice the clouds. Listen to the wind. There is no limit to what you can notice. You can look at my Instagram page to see what I notice on my medicine walks. It's the same walk every day, but there is always something new to notice. It's a new day. And you are new to each other.

As you continue to practice your medicine walk, you see the world as a reflection of yourself. It's always okay to feel your feelings. But try to walk those feelings into a natural setting and set your intention to breathe into them. Allow them to move through you and inform you. What is triggering you? What is the root cause or original wound creating the vibration of anger in your body?

You have the answers to your questions. You know your wounds, have the diagnosis to treat your disease, and are your own healer. Walk with your questions. Breathe into your emotions. Observe your surroundings and open yourself to how they reflect your mind. What reality are you projecting? What dream are you creating with your words? It's all inside you. The journey within yourself is inevitable. Start now. Walk there. If you want help, I'm here—until I'm not.

I'm Atlantis Wolf, and I believe in you.

Atlantis Wolf is a Master Shamanic Breathwork facilitator and guide who helps people take the next step after they've had an unusual, mystical, or spiritual experience. She thinks of it as stepping into your labyrinth and walking back out with you.

As a licensed medical massage therapist, shamanic life coach, and emotional release therapist, she works with people in chronic pain. Her joy is connecting people to their spiritual counterparts using guided drumming meditations, Shamanic Breathwork ceremonies, and fire circles.

She was spiritually asleep until her mother's death awakened her gifts to communicate with spiritual beings, power animals, and galactic dragons. She remembers her past lives as an Egyptian healer, Toltec curandera, and Ayurvedic traveling shaman. She believes everyone has the capacity to be guided into their own transformational healing journey.

Atlantis grew up on a single-lane dirt road in rural Ohio, walking in the woods, whistling to birds, and asking: *Why am I here on Earth? What is calling me today?* She continues to walk to the trees at sunrise almost every day (except if it's sleeting) to listen to nature's reply.

She holds dual degrees in Civil Engineering and English and has worked as an environmental engineer, technical writer, franchise store owner, business analyst, project manager, licensed massage therapist, certified Emotion Code practitioner, marketing consultant, and entrepreneur.

Atlantis is a certified Master Shamanic Breathwork facilitator and ordained Shamanic Minister by Linda Star Wolf, Founder of Venus Rising Association for Transformation and Seneca Wolf Clan lineage keeper. She is a certified Reiki Master by William Lee Rand, founder of the International Center for Reiki Training.

Atlantis is available for retreats, podcast interviews, and her favorite ceremony - Shamanic Breathwork and Cacao & Ecstatic Dance.

Connect with Atlantis:

Website: AtlantisWolf.com

Email: DragonMedicineWoman@gmail.com

YouTube: Atlantis Wolf

Instagram: @DragonMedicineWoman

You can't choose your moment of clarity.

~ M.E. Zondra

CHAPTER 5

FORCE OF NATURE

BURST OPEN YOUR TRUE ENERGY

Eliza James

My Story

I am a boxer, baby!
I lace up my boxing shoes.
My feet are lit and so is my path.

It is fucking early. I'm awakened from a deep sleep by an alarm. BAM!

It's time to break out of the dream world, where I do my best work, and bring these gifts into the physical world.

I am ready. I was born for this.

I find my way through the dark to turn on the lights. I pour myself a cup of hot coffee and sit in the stillness of the morning. I'm instantly filled with a deep sense of gratitude and great purpose. My early rising to the day supports my dedication and devotion to the life I've been gifted to lead and influence.

In here lives this depth of knowing; this is the one shot I've got. This is my first and last day. I visualize how I'll touch life today. My stomach turns with aliveness and excitement for the thrill of this energy exchange. My constant companion is my question:

What matters most, and how will I make that into physical matter?

My life force starts to break up the darkness of the night while shining light on the morning. My eyes start to twinkle with the stars from the cosmos; I can see more. My smile becomes bigger. My awakened dreams come to life. My heart opens and starts to pound with the eight billion beating hearts of Mother Earth.

I am alivened and enlightened.
It is time to take it to the streets, this is the workout of my life.
There is much work to do.
My medium is boxing.

As I turn the knob to open the closed door, I grab the most integral instrument, my magical tool belt. Its contents assist me in the measurement of what I value most. To the untrained eye, this is just a bag of rocks. It's a container of magical crystals from the Earth and powerful invisible energy I've blended from information on the coordinates of space and time. I use this wise energy of the unconscious with the intent of bringing it to consciousness.

I pair this with the intelligent energy of the heart's consciousness.
The universal most powerful force.
The frequency of the universal mother is nurturing and protective.

I raise my vibrations; joy, and enthusiasm are my fuel. Now full, I clip this on my waist. I open the door; roadwork is the first part of my practice as a boxer.

One foot in front of the other, I'm on my way to the boxing studio.

It's an eight-mile round trip to the boxing studio. Willing to go to any lengths, I go the distance. As I run through the quiet neighborhoods, I pass by all the people sleeping and wonder: *Am I the only one awake?*

The moon pours down her wisdom and her reflection now guides my path. My stride picks up and it's rhythmic with her waxing and waning, connecting my intuition. I drop deeper into my body and the depth of feeling offered here. I want to bring this feeling with me to my work. I have the eye of the tiger and the heart of the lion. I know that true strength comes from vulnerability and that I'm also a human being.

I will be brave enough to get to the heart of the matter.
My 10,000 hours turn into a mission.

My warm heart and the fire in my soul assist me on the cold winter morning.

Finally, I arrive at the boxing studio where I'm always greeted by a street cat named Scrappy. The whole place is illuminated by the cross I put on the building. There's a door; I have the key; I open it. The boxing bags are swaying, and the walls are painted. There's a powerful energy in this space.

Before I train anyone, I must train myself. I turn the music on and pull out some boxing wraps. There's a great sense of pride in wrapping my own hands for support with the wraps I created as the first female in history with a boxing brand.

I step over to the mirror to begin the next part of my practice, shadowboxing.

Shadowboxing is where a boxer practices their discipline in front of the mirror, like a dancer. I'm a southpaw, but I know how important it is to practice on both sides to meet somewhere in the middle. I get in an athletic stance, keep my elbows in, tight fists, and cover my face. The music is playing in the background; I start to dance and stay light on my feet. My feet are planted, rooted in the fiery core of the earth. I'm grounded.

Jab.

Right hand.

Straight down the middle.

Back to my face.

Power and speed.

I catch my reflection in the mirror to check my form and start to question myself. My voice in my head becomes louder and drowns out the music. I start shadowboxing for real. In my reflection in the mirror, I see my dad's face.

His pain of losing his dad at three years old shows up. His heartbreak and worry as he took eight of his own kids at 28 years old and relocated as a single dad with a broken heart.

Jab! Jab! Jab!

His hard work ethic and great commitment to spiritual matters.

Jab! Jab! Jab!

His fear of death, his quiet power, he was frightening. His inability to manage his own emotions and always telling me not to be so sensitive and emotional. His great laugh. I sacrificed my life for him as a little girl. His brilliant innovative ideas; he was a visionary. I have so much in common with his pain and his gifts.

I start to bounce.

I want to make him proud, and I do not want to be like him at all.

I reset.

Keep practicing, Eliza. Keep practicing.

**A good song comes on. I see myself in the mirror.
I am sexy. I am strong. I am a boxer.**

Jab cross.

Jab cross.

Jab cross.

The music gets quieter. I hear myself.

Who are you? So, you are a boxer? What does this mean to you? I have to be somebody in this world to matter. Think outside the box. What really matters, Eliza? And what are you going to make into matter with your energy?

As a child, I always heard, "If I could bottle that energy you have, I would sell it."

Now you have bottled it. You are a boxer.
A champion.
What do you want to champion?

Keep breathing; stay in your base.
What will you do with this power and strength, Eliza?
Do you really want to train yourself to
power over people and knock their lights out?
I thought you were about turning the lights on in people.
How are you going to be a champion?
How are you not going to continue all the physical abuse,
and violence you experienced?
The brass knuckles you bore on your cheek now add a dimple to your smile.
Your nose has been broken so many times, it's even now.
Are you going to pick competition over love?

Keep working it out, Eliza. Keep working.
You must become stronger to influence non-violence
in the traditional sport of boxing.

Back to the mirror.

Jab cross hook.

Jab cross hook.

You are a girl. What do you want to box for?

I suddenly see my mom in the reflection of the mirror. I feel her energy of being insignificant and dismissed. She had 12 kids and died at the age of 45.

I feel insignificant and dismissed. I feel the oppression of all women.

Slip.

Duck.

Weave.

Jab cross hook.

> *Stop beating yourself up, Eliza! Keep practicing!*
> *Build yourself up, and learn to love yourself while living your life well,*
> *in honor of your mom who did not get the chance.*
> *You are all heart. When the pain hits, the plans do not change.*

Keep breathing, keep healing.

> *You are powerful. You matter.*
> *With your great strength,*
> *you can show other women they have great power too.*
> *Keep healing, keep practicing.*
> *Keep working, Eliza. We are rising.*

Jab cross hook upper.

> *You are killing it, Eliza! What are you trying to kill, Eliza?*
> *Are you afraid to die or are you afraid to truly live?*
> *You have great gifts.*
> *You must learn how to live with them in this world even if they're different.*
> *It's okay to be different.*
> *You believe in the invisible energy of all times; you believe in magic.*

Jab.

Slip.

Uppercut.

Light on your toes!

> *What is your worth? What is your life's work worth?*
> *What matters? What is the matter?*
> *You have already died from cancer at 35,*
> *you know what it means to come back to life and bring more gifts.*

> *Keep breathing. Keep fighting for life.*

> *No fear here, no fear here.*

You got this.

Now go hit the bag. Release your tension.
Heal your wounds and fight for what you think matters most.
Bring real love and magic into this world.

Work that bag, don't let that bag work you. Work through the pain. Do not live your life through your wounds.

Get back to the light. Let the light be what heals those wounds. Light. Fast. Hits. Power!

I'm out of breath. My body has been exhausted from its work. I lay down on the cold, hard floor. I feel complete, whole. I'm filled with the energy of all time and people. Sweat turns into steam that rises from the top of my head as it settles.

My breathing slows down and becomes deeper. Peace comes over me. I suddenly see this lit ball of life in my hands. It's glowing; it's my life force. I marvel at its supernatural magic. This is my energy. This is what I've been preserving my whole life and I will never extinguish the light from it.

My questions are the answers themselves.

What matters most and what I will make into matter. I am fully present. This is the gift. It's simple but not simple-minded.

I am ready to offer this to the world.

I rise, stand tall in my true power, ready to train the people.

It's still early in the morning; the sun is now bursting its way through. Several people start to walk down the alley. They too, are being pulled to their personal power. Their eyes are still sleepy and start to open in their search for what they are seeking. They listen to their hearts and let the vibrational beat of all hearts lead them to the door.

"Good morning, Wolfie. How are you, Lamb? What's up, Doc? Hi, 11:11."

Most of my clients have nicknames and I have memorized their phone numbers by heart. I'm committed to making real connections while having human contact. My sober eyes look deep into theirs. I see them. I am here—heart forward.

My biggest muscle is my heart, and it greets them first thing.

I give them a strong hug; I know the journey they've been on.

They open the door to our spiritual playground. The place is packed; I wonder if I'm able to play with so many others at one time because I was raised with a team of heroes: my siblings. Here we can hold the opposites. Pain and joy, work and rest, weakness and strength, darkness and light, male and female. This is our practice. It takes repetition after repetition to build our practice into practical life.

We are spiritual scientists practicing our method over and over again until we've built a foundation of trust through self. No one can do the workout but them, but they don't have to do it alone. My plan is loose, it stays new and I allow it to evolve naturally.

I hold the boxing mitts for them now. It's time they see their true power from their work. Part of what's driving them is their pain. They move through the awkwardness of their new practice.

Their hits are powerful, their truth is clumsy.
Their voices are weak but get stronger as they learn to speak.
They are now my teacher; they show me what brave looks like.

It's like physics; they continue with curiosity to see what they'll discover by striking fiery hit after hit. I'm a conductor, a conduit of light. I become their mirror and reflect their pain and power back to them. I'm their muse; I dare them to give me all that they've got. I scare the shit out of them while asking them what their truth is.

My vision is clear, there is a special harmony of sensitivity and strength that allows them to fully show up.

"Give me all your power!"

"Is that all you've got?"

"Go deeper!"

"Stay in your base."

"Show me what you're made of."

"Make a name for yourself."

"You matter."

"Go hit that bag. Hit it until you don't see the other person's face on it anymore. Go deeper. Get to yourself. It's your turn. Bring yourself back to life."

"Rise!"

"Rise!"

"Power!"

For the next part of their practice, I lead them through a cross-training program. They build a relationship with their body as they endure pain much like the ecstasy and agony of giving birth. The biology of breaking down muscle fibers is a birthing similar in nature. We do a signature workout called Chance. I named it after my son.

The clock is set.

"Eight, nine, ten. . .and we go!"

Work.

Pain.

Gain.

"Finish strong!"

Most do not make it, but they know sometimes it takes five years to complete a workout. Their hard work is R-E-S-P-E-C-T and they find out what it means to me. They are now lying on the floor, their hearts beating out of their chests. They feel like they almost died but now feel more alive than they have ever felt.

They lay with their arms spread, hands wide open, and are now more connected to their breath, realizing this is what led them through the workout. Their body has been exhausted of all its armor and they feel completely open. They can allow something deeper to come in.

It's now my turn to use this inlet to speak to what matters most.

This is our house.
This building we are in used to be the 22nd Liquor Store.
It is now Boxing is for Girls.
We are drinking from a different kind of spirits.

The Medicine

I pull out my spiritual readings. Scrappy, the street cat, our spiritual advisor, saunters in as he feels the energy has shifted. He purrs and rubs his healing vibrations up against you. You pet him. He heals you. You let him.

Today, I speak to you about death.

I prepare you for your deathbed. I begin with your breath. I explain to you that your breath is the first and last thing you will do and it is oftentimes the thing that is most ignored during your life.

I present the questions:

"What will you bring with you when you go out into the world?"
"What will you make into matter?"

You know a little bit about death now because you just survived the workout.

I remind you to face your fears so you can start truly living.

The Earth is the heart of the cosmos.

You're now more conscious of your ability to lead with your heart and put feelings back into life. You know we're not machines.

Strength comes from being vulnerable.
I know the undertaking and incredible responsibility of being a
spiritual warrior.
I am this. What you see in me, you, too, are it. We are one.
I stick to my formula 1 + 1 = One.

As I run home, the crystals become the grid to life. I go over my day and go through my magical tool belt checklist.

Time is relative. Healing does not take time. Healing takes healing.
I heal myself and simultaneously, I heal others.

The street I'm running on becomes expansive and turns into my quantum field. Suddenly, I see my past self and I say thank you to her for the innocence and purity in her power to stay committed to love while she endured all the pain. I see my present self and say, "You are doing it; you are carrying the lessons. You're making transformations; all this pain was not in vain, and I wouldn't take it away for anything." This is the very reason why I can hold the mitts for a six-foot-eight, 400-pound heavyweight champion who is eating himself to death and I don't get hurt. I'm a shapeshifter; I become all energy. Mine, his, and of all times.

In the quantum, I can connect to all the great teachers who've passed. I become this unstoppable force of infinite wisdom and power. This is where I hold the hand of the dead. My future self reaches her hand towards my present self, I take it and say, "Let's go! I trust you. I am home."

Movement is medicine; stillness is pure magic.
I lay my body down to rest and restore. I quiet my mind.
I drop into my sacred heart space, my soulmate.
I feel eternal love living here, where everything is okay.
I start to rest, I sleep soundly, peacefully, I keep my dreams awake.
My subconscious plays out the stories of the wounds again,
my healing continues.
I also receive prescient messages that I will continue to integrate.

I'm awakened by an alarm. BAM! Still, I rise.
I begin with the end in mind. I do it all over again.

As I leave the studio to go home, I pause in gratitude at the purple eight-foot steel cross lit on the building. Creativity has always been a part of my healing process. I created this art piece in honor of Anna, grandmother to Jesus. The symbolism is a reminder of my dedication to light conception. I also feel the energy of my great-grandmother Kissiah. She donated land for a church and cemetery still standing today and where she is laid to rest. These two women I deeply know but have never met. Most of what I know I never had to be taught. It's in my very cellular makeup, in my blood, in my genes. I draw from the source of their strength and thank them for making my life into an answered prayer.

My medicine is my decision.
In my decision is my commitment.
In my commitment is my plan.
In my plan is my heart.
In my heart is my pain
In my pain is my power.

Connect with **Eliza James** at:

Website: https://boxingisforgirls.com/

Instagram: https://www.instagram.com/boxingisforgirls/

Facebook: https://www.facebook.com/BoxingIsForGirls

"Movement is medicine, stillness is pure magic."

~ Eliza James

CHAPTER 6

DRAWING A BLANK

REDESIGNING YOURSELF, YOUR THOUGHTS, AND YOUR INNER DIALOGUE

Rachelle Golding

*You are only ever at your worst
the first time you try something new*

~ unknown

My Story

I remember thinking to myself as I spoke to Brian, my manager at the time: *Why did I have to open my mouth? Why couldn't I just lie down and take it? Was I being emotional and irrational? Not really. She had it coming.*

Releasing an audible sigh and rubbing my eyes, I thought: *I probably did it because I wanted her to suffer, to be in just as much pain as I was in.*

Bringing myself back to the present conversation, I heard Brian asking if I was sure I wanted to follow through with my formal complaint about the warehouse supervisor, Fiona. He advised me that it would become part of both our employee records and once entered, there would be no rescinding of my complaint. I recall saying, "Yes, I'm sure," as I felt the lump in my throat finding its resting place in the pit of my stomach.

Oh God, Rachelle, you're in deep shit now! I kept telling myself this as I attempted to keep the tears from flowing and my voice from shaking.

Brian then asked me to go over what happened the day prior to ensure there was a proper record of the event. Still feeling very raw and heartsick, I contemplated the rolling sensation of nausea.

Am I feeling sick because I don't want Brian to think less of me or because I know I am in trouble?

Giving my head a shake, I was touching on something so tender, coupled with the unhealthy compulsion to ensure everyone liked me. *Now isn't the time to be a self-reflective dummy.* My stress-triggered system was going into shutdown mode. With a trembling hand, I wiped away tears I didn't give permission to fall. *When did I start crying again?*

Without realizing how long I paused, Brian chimed in to indicate he had spoken with Fiona the morning prior, letting her know I suffered a grave family loss of three relatives in a house fire overnight, and as such, the schedule was changing to have me work the sales floor rather than in the warehouse.

Thankful for the prompt, I began recounting how I had been left to myself most of the day and it wasn't until closer to the end of my shift that Fiona paged me to call the warehouse. I recited the conversation between Fiona and myself after the page:

"I need you in the warehouse now!" Fiona barked through the phone.

Emotionally exhausted and physically depleted, I sighed, "Okay, I will finish up with the last of the stock that I have, then I will head back."

"No! You will come here now." Fiona growled through the receiver.

With apprehension growing in my chest and ringing in my ear, I barked back, "No. I will finish with the stock and then I will head to the warehouse."

As I recapped the conversation to Brian, I vividly remember the creeping sensation of foreboding, like that of a looming storm, while on the phone with Fiona. From the moment I heard her voice to the abruptness of her hanging up on me mid-sentence. I had begun mentally preparing myself for the fight I knew was coming.

She's going to start yelling at me; I just know it. What am I going to do? I should go hide in the bathroom. No, she will just hunt me down regardless of where I try to hide. I should yell right back at her, but I don't want to cause a scene. What should I say?

I went on to explain how after the conversation, I made my way back to where I was working with tightness blooming in my chest. I finished with the last stock when I felt a hand grip the back of my arm. I recalled what Fiona said through gritted teeth, "I said to come back to the warehouse. Now." She then gripped my arm tighter and began to pull me in the direction of the warehouse. I remarked to Brian how it took significant effort, but I wrenched my arm free. At that moment, I felt a flood of adrenaline wash through my body. I saw red; I was ready for war.

I told Brian what I was thinking on the walk back to the warehouse.

How dare she touch me! What right does she have to invade my space? Un-fucking believable! Rachelle, just breathe. Try to remain calm. There is no point in making the situation worse than it is going to be. No, fuck that! She shouldn't have grabbed me like that.

I deliberately kept the less-than-work-appropriate thoughts out of my conversation with Brian. I remember feeling so small, ashamed, and disappointed in myself when I recounted how the conversation with Fiona went in the warehouse.

"How dare you be so disrespectful. When I order you to do something, your role is to listen!" Fiona snarled.

"Me being disrespectful. That is hardly the case here, Fiona," I replied. I tried to continue speaking, remaining as calm as I could only to have her speak over me,

"Oh yes, it is. I'm the warehouse supervisor which makes me your superior. You listen to me," she spat, and continuing she asked, "What is your problem with me?"

With my cheeks burning and my heart pounding I screamed, "Fiona, you're a bitch! No one likes you." As the words left my lips, the bloodthirsty warrior who walked into the warehouse disguised as Rachelle took her shot. We both stood stunned in silence, staring at one another, not believing the fierce words that escaped my lips.

At this point in the conversation with Brian, I took ownership of my part in the conflict. As I wiped away yet more rogue tears, I thought: *Well, there you go, you are in deep shit now. He now knows you called her a bitch. Fuck, I'm probably going to get reprimanded as bad or worse than Fiona.*

I told him I tried to remove myself from the situation by leaving for the day. However, Fiona was insistent on engaging further in the conflict, continuing to yell insults at me, all the while blocking my only exit. Terrifying thoughts flooded my mind, feeling like a caged and panicked animal attempting to flee its captor. *I need out! I can't breathe! I need air! Oh God, I'm trapped!* I continued to explain that I had to physically remove her from in front of the door in order to escape.

I felt incredibly distraught knowing until that point in my life, I had never been so angry as to lose my cool in that fashion, to spew something so deliberately venomous at another person. It was shortly after this incident (and much to my relief) that I was transferred to another store location in my hometown of Cranbrook, British Columbia. It was back in Cranbrook where I found a posting that read: *"The Ascension Handbook: How to Navigate your Spirit in this Human Experience."* It was as if the Universe heard the yearning within my soul when I read the posting, answering with smooth tones, letting me know I was on the right track. The moment I read those words, I knew my life was never going to be the same.

Little did I know what a magical, miraculous, and wonderful journey of self-discovery it would send me on, and what amazing lessons, growth, and introspection it would unfurl within me. I didn't know how impactful the ever-evolving teachings would be on my perception of what it is to truly listen, reflect, and understand inner dialogues, and what it is to be an observer of our inner conversations. I would learn to explore the teachings of self-discovery and make sense of the conversation in my head during the storm I had weathered, named Fiona.

The Medicine

My dearest reader,

I commend you for the strength to hold yourself in a space that'll surely crack you open. I commend you for appreciating the beauty of being raw and vulnerable, opening yourself up to allowing a deep healing process to begin. As well, I'd also like to extend my gratitude to you for reading my story, and for holding space for me while I shared this triggering ordeal. I thank you for taking the leap with us into this sacred container which is this book.

Take a moment to listen to what kind of conversation you're having with yourself right now, at this very moment. Where are your thoughts taking you and what type of physical reaction are you having in your body? Do you feel tension anywhere in your body? What did my story trigger in you? Are your thoughts now racing or are they circling around a singular issue? Are you obsessing over a person, project, or situation you had no control over? What about your breathing? Is it shallow and quick? Now dip down into your heart space by straightening your back and taking three big, slow lung-expanding breaths. Listen to how quiet and calm it is here. Take another three big expansive breaths. How does your body feel now? Do you still feel that tension, or has it eased? Simply observe.

Let us now travel to where we can gain a meaningful understanding of the relationship within ourselves. The personal abode I speak of within is a sacred place that no other person can hold captive. I speak of our heart space, the very center of our physical body. In chakra work, I believe the heart space is where the dense physical energy centers twirl and blend with the spiritual energy centers. It's in our heart space that, when opened and attuned to a higher vibration, leads to miraculous things. It's in this place where we can flush out all that doesn't serve to create a blank canvas to redesign ourselves—giving way to a shift in the frequency of our inner dialogue.

It's an odd concept, the idea that we all have an inner monologue happening that can manifest itself into the physical world. For many, myself included, it's typically a fear-based tug-of-war. Subsequently, it brings down our frequency to a much denser level. The question is, at what point did we allow ourselves to become slaves to its barrage of negativity and just accept it? When did we allow this negative little beasty, which I will refer to as Ego, to run so rampant? So constant is the chatter that over time it erodes us and can bring about episodes of anxiety and depression. The source of Ego is complex and can come from different experiences we've accumulated over our lifetime, and it'll look different for all of us.

The source of Ego can be any traumas, rejections, or concessions we've made with ourselves. To explore the depths to which the Ego has gone, it's important that we go into our heart space. This gives us the opportunity to hold ourselves in a safe container and to practice quieting the mind. By holding space for ourselves, we can then work towards the next step in our healing journey. The next step is being an observer of our inner dialogues, a stalker of ourselves, if you will. This means we must watch our thoughts without judgment or animosity.

When we take the position of a stalker to our inner dialogue, it's incredible what patterns of fear-based thoughts are caught. Fearful thinking could resemble thoughts like: *There are so many incredible contributing authors to this book. I am not good enough to be among them.* Or, *I don't have anything to offer; why bother?* Those are exactly the thoughts I had floating around while writing this. However, it presented a wonderful opportunity to drop into that heart space, to catch those thoughts, examine them at length, and release them without judgment. The ability to recognize this unhealthy train of thoughts is important because it stops the cascading effect of self-doubt paralysis. It offers me the room to shift my perception of how I view myself versus how I think the world perceives me. The practice I describe above may appear on the surface to be an easy task, but as the saying goes, it is easier said than done.

Being our own heart space stalker takes work. It's like any other muscle in the body. It requires care and attention to remain flexible. For our heart space to remain healthy and perform effectively it must be exercised regularly to reach a higher vibrational level. Unlike traditional exercises for the body, attuning your heart space can take on many different consciously created daily practices. It could be journaling snips of the inner dialogues that occurred throughout the day, visualizations, meditation, connecting with like-minded people, or it could even be as simple as small acts of kindness.

My favorite way to keep the heart space in shape is with meditation. For me, meditation is a quiet walk out in nature with my dogs. Another way is to keep my child-like sense of wonder alive, stopping to admire a neat rock or finding dinosaur shapes amongst the clouds. Most important of all has been finding my tribe. To be among people willing to meet me at my level but push me just that little bit outside of my comfort zone, all the while respecting my boundaries.

The beauty of creating daily practices is that over time they become unconscious, positive habits. It becomes easier to take a step back and observe the conversations we have within ourselves, to recognize thoughts that do not serve any purpose but create fear and anxiety. These positive habits we construct allow for deeper exploration of the traumas, rejections, or concessions we've made with ourselves. By holding ourselves in a place of love we can be curious and open while exploring, without fear of re-traumatizing. It creates a foundation for you to build a healthier version of yourself. To catch yourself when you begin to allow old habits to creep back in.

So, what does all this mean for you, my dearest reader? Where do we go from here? Well, that's the beauty of this journey. It's yours to make of it what you wish. My words are yours now to mold and shape into what resonates deepest with you. They may be the launch pad that shoots you into a previously unexplored universe, or perhaps they will slip in and out of your consciousness like a gentle stream trickling down the mountainside. Either path is no more right or wrong than the other. Do not be discouraged if it's difficult at the beginning. These practices take time to hone. Always remember that you are only at your worst the very first time you try something new.

Rachelle Golding is a Canadian rocky mountain goddess. She is a loving wife to her high school sweetheart and fur-mother to two rambunctious canines and three mischievous felines. She is a court clerk with the Court Service Branch, a sector within the British Columbian Government. She is actively involved as a member of a multitude of health and wellness committees within the Court Service Branch organization. She walks in both the corporate world and the spiritual world with ease. Rachelle is a dedicated Reiki Master through the Usui System of Natural Healing. Her work with Angel has allowed her the honor of being one of the first priestesses initiates of the Nina Songo Energy Medicine Mystery School. As well, Rachelle is a practicing physical medium who believes when Spirit comes knocking, it's time to get rocking. With her zest for life and thirst for continued healing, she brings a ray of sunshine to every encounter.

Contact with Rachelle at:

Instagram: @etherealpearls

Facebook: https://www.facebook.com/etherealpearls

"Being our own heart space stalker takes work.
It's like any other muscles in the body."

~ Rachelle Golding

CHAPTER 7

THE FORGOTTEN SELF

AND HOW TO REMEMBER HER

Daphne Paras, MSEd

My Story

I was lying in the firm hotel bed, alone, with thoughts racing through my mind: *Am I truly dying? Will I see my girls again? I am so glad I got the medical evacuation insurance. Just hang on until one o'clock. You got to make it to one.*

One o'clock came and the door opened. Silent, he went to the bathroom and then to the safe to check his iPad. Standing there, he read his emails, not even noticing my presence in the room.

What the fuck? Where are my children? Did you actually leave them alone at a pool in Mexico? Are you going to come and see me before I die?

I felt my blood pressure rising. Suddenly, I felt alive again.

I shouted with an energy I didn't even know I had, "What the fuck is wrong with you? I don't have a friend on Earth that wouldn't come straight to my bedside."

Flustered, he stared blankly at me.

The heartbreak and the anger—those moments—brought me back to life that day.

For the next three weeks, the tears I held in for so long streamed like a steady flowing river. The awakening was happening. Everything I held in and pretended was okay surfaced like an erupting volcano.

What the hell happened that day at Coba? What spirits woke me? What Universal powers are at play?

It started just like every other family vacation I planned, at least two weeks away to coerce my husband into spending time with his family. Beautiful pictures were taken of us all looking perfectly happy, with coordinated outfits, excursions, and everything seamlessly planned and executed.

We had never ventured to the pyramids before. I negotiated one family vacation a year. The rest of the trips were girls only. I convinced myself this was just fine and felt immense gratitude for traveling the world with my daughters.

We started out early to beat the heat, but by the time we reached the pyramid at Coba, the sun was scorching. We finally reached the top and I knew we'd have to come back down soon, as there was no shade. It felt like we climbed up next to the sun. We peered over the edge, *oh fuck, that is really steep!* I assured them we could do this and carefully, step by step, backward, we navigated our way down.

Safe.

We were safer than I thought. We were protected. Looking back, I know the ancients were with me, I know they knew there was something much greater for my life and purpose, and they sure brought it.

I made a promise that I'd never put my girls through a divorce. I wouldn't let them experience the pain I did as a child. Then there was one moment, and it arrived on my doorstep like a ton of bricks: *What if one of them comes to me at almost 40, crying, in despair, telling me they were so lonely and in a loveless and sexless marriage?* A veil lifted; I'd be responsible, as that's the only example I've ever shown them. Once I saw that vision, I could not unsee it.

No more. We either change our marriage, or we end it.

If I had enough courage to really look at myself, I wouldn't have recognized who I had become. I had forgotten an entire self, completely buried her away to protect her.

Those tears? I couldn't stop them; I couldn't hide them; they were determined. I surrendered, over and over again. It felt like the ultimate act of vulnerability.

I had to pick the girls up at their mini-school and see the other moms, "Yes, I'm okay, maybe finally okay. I think I just held them in for too long." Everyone seemed to understand. Some joined me, others hugged me, and some confided their deepest secrets to me.

I had dinner plans with a friend and I didn't cancel. "I have these tears that just want to flow and I can't stop them, so if you are okay with that, we can keep our plans." He sat next to me in my car, just being with me as I drove, and let those tears run.

I didn't judge them; I didn't question them. I allowed them. There was nothing else I could do. They trained me quickly.

I barely saw my husband; his travel kept him away for almost the entire three weeks, which was common. I had little faith we could shift. He couldn't be with the tears anyway; he didn't know me that way. No one did.

I started opening up to a few close friends about the despair I had denied. My perfect life wasn't so perfect. Up until this point, I couldn't see it; I wouldn't see it. I was determined to make my life work the way I believed it should.

Another dear friend gifted me a session with an intuitive. The first sentence she spoke after "hello" was, "This separation will be a good thing."

What? Who told her this? Oh, my friend had to have filled her in.

Nope. The guides spoke to her. *Okay, lady, you have my full attention.*

"Harness your goddess energy," she said calmly, "that is your key."

Well great, what the fuck does that mean?

I began searching for answers. I needed wisdom, a roadmap, guidance, call it whatever you like. I was a sponge trying to soak up anything I could to soothe my soul, to give me an explanation of what was happening to me and how to move through it.

I was in the laundry room of a ski rental in Colorado. I left the girls and my dad upstairs. I was having an epic release. My dad couldn't be with my tears either. I was getting it out on the phone with a friend and he tells me, "This is your return to Uranus, your midline. When you're not living in accord with your higher purpose, the Universe will conspire to change it. That's all."

That's all? Well, this makes perfect sense, but can the Universe be a bit gentler on me? No, of course not. It tried the gentle route, the knocking on my door, and I didn't listen. Or I couldn't hear it.

My husband discovered some text messages while I was away. There was a man I had several dinners with, with my husband's consent and knowledge. It was during that time that I really discovered he didn't care what I did or whom I did it with.

Throughout our marriage, about once a year, I broke down in despair. I pleaded, "Why won't you touch me? What is wrong with me? I need touch. I need sex. I need affection." It didn't make a difference.

We tried counseling. I tried being the perfect wife. The house was spotless, the girls were well-behaved, and I was the prettiest I could be.

I even asked for an open marriage once. I thought that if maybe I could get one need met, I could survive staying. I created stories: *Maybe he doesn't respect me staying home, maybe he doesn't like my post-baby body, maybe he's having an affair. . .maybe, maybe, maybe.*

In those texts he found, there was some PG-13 flirting. He also read my words, "I will not cheat on my husband, it's not who I am, but I'd be interested in exploring dating you if and when we separated."

The fear kicked in full throttle for him, and he told me he'd fight to the ends of the Earth to save our marriage. *Okay, let's try this!*

I returned from Colorado almost exactly four weeks after climbing Coba, to the man I fell in love with—attentive, interested, and sexual.

The next 14 months became the most amazing, challenging, and heart-breaking time of my life. He connected, and then completely disconnected, ten times over those 14 months. Each time the connection period shortened; each time my heart was ripped open deeper.

My heart, could you still be broken even more? Or are you breaking open so deeply that you can expand more than you ever have?

It was as if a light switch was flicked on and off. On, he was the man I fell in love with. Off, he was the cold disconnected stranger who didn't even see me walk by him fully naked.

We went through three different therapists. He didn't see a problem. I spent so much life force energy wondering about him not being able to meet my needs. *Is he unable? Or just unwilling?* At the end of the day, it didn't matter. My needs were so far from being met.

I was attending workshops for myself and gaining certifications to embody my goddess energy and teach others how to do so. I became a work in progress, rather than a pretty finished product. I owned it. I talked about my journey, my despair, and my heartache.

We returned to Hawaii, where he asked me to marry him again. I couldn't. I compromised on a commitment ceremony where I spoke of commitments I could honor, being the best me possible, doing the work, and being accountable.

That night at dinner, he leaned over to me and whispered in my ear, "I forgot to say my commitments, didn't I?" With the familiar heartbreak, I replied, "Yes, you are correct." I wish I could say I was surprised.

The next morning, we were at breakfast. The waitress had the name of his ex-wife. It sparked a conversation about their wedding. The girls and I were learning about his previous life. When I pressed for the location, he reminded me we'd been there together, just five months before. In fact, I was in such awe of the hotel that I exclaimed, "Could you imagine getting married here?!"

I circled back, "When I said, 'could you imagine getting married here,' and you said 'yeah,' I didn't realize it was because you actually did get married there."

"Daph, I honestly didn't even connect the two until just now."

I believed him. He was that disconnected. Our third therapist believed he had an addiction to disconnection. *Well, that certainly explains a few things.*

You see, I remember every place I've ever kissed someone, and definitely every bigger moment. But we were different. I lived in a place of connectedness and vulnerability, with my heart open, or at least I tried.

I took my rings off that day, and never put them back on. I asked him to move out when we returned home.

Oh my heart, my brave and terrified heart. What have I done?

In a matter of days, I helped him find an apartment. A shaman I worked with described the energy of him coming and going like a 747 jet taking off and landing. The jet took off, a cloud lifted from the house, and it never landed there again.

The next phase of work began—uncovering the depths of rejection and healing it.

The first time I imagined being sexual with another human, my heart stopped. I was now months away from turning 40. I hadn't been sexual with another since my 20s. The fear, the contraction, it was paralyzing.

What has happened to me? Where did that vibrant, sexual, confident woman go? It was as if I had completely forgotten an entire self. *How do I remember her?*

I started my own personal journey, Friday night date nights, where I dated myself. I cooked a gourmet dinner for one, watched a scary movie, took a Zumba class, dove into sacred self-pleasuring, and sometimes did all of them!

Somewhere on this journey, I learned that when we sever our connection to our sexuality, we cut off our life force energy. Literally, as women, our womb space creates life. So many of us, from one sort of trauma or another, sever that connection. It made so much sense to me and I realized how severing this connection was such a punishment to myself and the world around me. I was determined to repair it.

After all, when we're in alignment with our sexuality, we show up differently in the world; at the grocery store, as a mom, as a boss babe. You know the women I'm talking about—fully present in their bodies, with a certain confidence about them, aware of the intricacies that light them up. I wanted in on that!

I started with a very intentional self-pleasure practice, relearning my body as if I was brand new to her and she was brand new to me. I learned what she liked, what she felt like, and even what she looked like. I made peace with her, acknowledging the changes she endured and feats she accomplished, loving her, over and over again.

When the time felt right, I called in partners. I knew I needed my focus to be on my girls, and that the road ahead would be expansive and challenging. I had lovers who were gentle, amazing, and loving. Most of all, they accepted where I was on my journey, and celebrated me for it.

I continued facilitating workshops and grew my offerings. The more I spoke my truth, the more the collective healed with me.

As I learned of so many women who also severed their connection to their sacred sexuality, my flame grew for this underserved and rarely talked about phenomenon.

I set out to shift my mind, body, and spirit. My core belief is that each and every one of us is born with a set of gifts. Our job is to uncover those gifts and use them to better this world. As I grew further into alignment with my gifts, I felt all the support I needed. The Universe was cheering me on every step of the way. I woke up and asked, "What magic is going to happen today?" And the magic happened.

The Medicine

I developed many practices to thrive.

Return to your body. Surrender. Connect. Listen. Heal. Repeat. These were the words that I lived by.

My mind was busier than ever. Constantly trying to solve every possible dilemma. I felt like a crazy person. The controller in me was in charge, and the more I tried to control, the less control I felt.

Gratitude.

I wrote it on sticky notes and placed them all over my home, two still hang to this day.

I set up a gratitude reminder on my phone to alert me every 30 minutes of my awake hours. Whenever those bells would chime, no matter what I was doing or who I was with, I stopped, placed my hand firmly on my heart, and said at least one thing I was thankful for. When I was with others I simply asked, "Would you like to join me in a moment of gratitude?" The response was always an excited "Yes!" I trained myself. After a few weeks, when my disaster mind ran on and on, I could just stop, place my hand on my heart, and shift into my body. As I continued practicing shifting out of the fear from my mind into the magic of my body, my heart expanded.

Self-pleasure.

My sexuality was poorly neglected for far too long. It was as if I took the rejection from my husband and used it to punish myself. I completely internalized it and even convinced myself I wasn't a sexual being anymore. It took me some time to feel sexual and connected to my body again.

Starting with my breath, I create an orb of light, breathing it into my root chakra. On the inhale, I run it up the spine of my body and on the exhale, down the front, creating a loop. I use the light to clear any blockages and stagnant energy. From there to the sacral chakra, solar plexus, heart, throat, third eye, and finally the crown chakra. I spend as much time as I need to at each chakra, using my breath, and the orb of light to clear. Each time, using my breath to take the orb all the way back down to my root chakra and loop it back up again.

I found it important to set up a sacred space and ritual for this. Sometimes just lighting a candle, other times starting with a bath and massaging delicious body butter into my skin with sensual music and essential oils diffusing.

Setting the intention to love and heal myself, to honor any and all feelings that would arise, to let go of any expectations, to have fun, and to be fully present.

I began to incorporate self-pleasure with this breathing and chakra clearing. Breast massage became an epic tool to open my heart. My breasts had an awakening of their own when they gave life to my daughters. Honoring and worshipping their power felt in total alignment with my goddess energy. I tried different toys to explore pleasure and different varieties of orgasms. A cervical orgasm? Yes, please!

Building up the pleasure as my breath moved throughout my body allowed me to be fully present in each chakra. I played with building that energy, then holding it as I reached the crown chakra, coordinating my climax with the crown, letting the energy explode from my head and into the Universe, and letting it rain back down onto my being–exquisite.

Return to your body. Surrender. Connect. Listen. Heal. Repeat—as many times over as you need.

Daphne leads people by igniting the fire within them. She has found great satisfaction in facilitating corporate and private workshops, as well as one-on-one coaching. She excels at holding space and guiding people deep into the wisdom of their bodies, where she believes the magic happens. Daphne leads by example, often citing she is both the teacher and the student, always on a mission to learn and expand more.

She has learned how to go deeper within herself, and in turn take others deeper using tools such as breathwork, meditation, and a variety of guided practices. She is passionate about helping women identify where trauma lives in the body and using pathways to clear and heal it.

Her journey led her to design and invent The Seeker, a sacred self-exploration and pleasure tool. She is on a mission to remove the shame and guilt and normalize open conversation and communication around sexuality. As well as inspire living in pleasure!

Daphne facilitates workshops around empowerment, reclaiming your voice, sexuality, and returning to your authentic self. One of her favorite experiences for helping people be fully present in their bodies is Firewalking. Her work as a firewalk Master allows her to certify instructors and facilitate workshops guiding people into their fears and across 1800-degree coals.

Daphne believes one of the greatest honors and responsibilities she has is guiding her teenage daughters. With loving, open communication and connection, her goal is to help them thrive and live without shame or guilt.

She is in a conscious partnership with a man who is her perfect mirror and lights her up entirely. She rests in the safety of the divine masculine to hold for her in all the ways she has needed to heal and fully bloom.

Connect with Daphne:

Website: www.sacredseeker.com

*"My core belief is that each and every one of us is born with
a set of gifts. Our job is to uncover those gifts and
use them to better this world."*

~ Daphne Paras

CHAPTER 8

THE SECRET OF HUMMING

HARNESSING THE POWER OF YOUR VOICE FOR PERSONAL TRANSFORMATION

Bradford W. Tilden, CMT, MM, UWT

"In the beginning was the Word, and the Word was with God, and the Word was God."

~ John 1:1

My Story

*In the beginning was the word...*I burst out laughing in the shower. Loud belly laughs. You know the type—the ones that make *your* sides hurt and make you gasp for breath. I was laughing because my spirit guides suggested I open this chapter with the above verse from the bible. It's the perfect verse in so many ways. It's a profound implication of the workings of manifestation, a reminder that we are God-like beings co-creating this shared reality, and tells us sound is the key.

I didn't grow up religious, although I was raised Congregationalist. As a child, I didn't get the concept of having an intermediary between myself and the divine source of creation. I was wired differently, and because of certain unique experiences I had as child, I became a seeker of spiritual truths at an early age.

I developed an authentic connection with the God of my understanding primarily through direct experiences. Great Spirit, as the natives put it, the "All," according to the ETs, and the Universe being my personal favorite, all speak of the same divine intelligence. Most importantly, I came to acknowledge we ourselves, are reflections and unique expressions of God.

"In the beginning was the word, and the word was...Hmmmm. Hmmmm. Hmmmm." Or, at least that is what it was for me.

These were the first sounds I made as I entered this world. I wasn't born crying. Instead, when they placed me in my mother's arms I began to hum. Not only that, my mother will tell you how all the doctors and nurses gathered around to listen to the miraculous humming baby.

For years I pondered what compelled me to hum as my first instinct upon entering this world. Was I simply content upon arrival? Was I giving my future self a signpost? Was I recreating the sensation of being in the womb? Was I intuitively counteracting the discordant buzz of the overhead fluorescent lighting? How would I know to do such a thing? What knowledge did I bring through with me? What is this secret of humming?

I used to think it peculiar and interesting that I attracted an audience with my humming within minutes of my birth. Now it makes complete sense, given the career I've built. As a professional sound healer, people gather around me to listen and receive the healing sounds of my angelic and shamanic vocal toning, humming and all.

Even though I was born with this vocal note-to-self, this beautiful openness, I wasn't always this aligned with my gift of healing vocal expression. I, too, experienced trauma as a child that disconnected me from my power. I remember vividly the moment I began to doubt myself.

I was an unabashed flamboyant young performer at seven years old. I loved to dance and sing along with my favorite songs. My song of choice at that time was *"Take My Breath Away"* by Berlin. I was being babysat by an older cousin. I was performing for her, swaying and singing with all my heart's content, lost in the reverie of sonic bliss, "Take my breath awaaaaay…"

When suddenly, I was snatched out of it by my cousin's sharp remark, "You're singing out of tune!" Maybe it wasn't intended to be harsh criticism, but her words pierced my heart and wounded my joy.

Was I singing out of tune? I didn't think so. It didn't sound like it to me. What if I've been singing out of tune this whole time and didn't realize it? I thought I was singing in tune!

These thoughts of self-criticism flooded my sensitive, impressionable mind. With one seemingly insignificant comment, the seeds of self-consciousness took root and my joy of singing began to slip away.

Singing in public became tentative after that, and my world made unsure.

Not long after, I experienced another trauma that silenced my voice from all public consumption for years to come. It was the proverbial middle school musical. I was cast as the lead tenor in a light-hearted parody called "Hey, George" by Elizabeth Peach and Sally McBride about George the knight who goes to slay the last dragon. I had to sing a tenor solo in front of the entire student body. Nervousness doesn't even come close to the anxiety my peer-pressured pre-pubescent self suffered before, during, and after that excruciating moment of torture. You see, the melody was written so there is a leap up whenever I had to sing "Hey–Geooooorge…" that went right into the top of my cracking vocal range. It was more terrifying and embarrassing for me than the real stage kiss I also had to give to the heroine later on after I saved her, and that says a lot!

That was the last time I sang publicly for 12 years.

Privately, however, my voice was free and creatively thriving. My falsetto voice was a place I adored exploring any chance I got. I was, and am still, an opera diva in the shower. During church services, I sang the soprano line to the hymns even though my mother would elbow me in the ribs every time I did. I mimicked sounds with my voice, inspired by Michael Winslow from his scene in the 1987 movie *SpaceBalls*.

I was fortunate to be born into a loud family. We all loved to scream, not in anger, but as a preferred means of communication. Instead of coming close to converse, we shouted to each other between two, and sometimes three, floors of our house. I also grew up surrounded by woods where I spent much of my time after school. When I heard the faint cry of my mother's voice from deep within the forest indicating dinner was ready, I shouted with all of my strength in response indicating I received her call. This is significant because I naturally kept my voice full, with the diaphragm, the seat of the power, engaged.

All of this and more became relevant once I discovered my voice as a healing tool. Upon reflection, I came to realize I developed and mastered the instrument of my voice my whole life, despite the public shaming I endured as a child. That is unique because many people shut their voices down. I work with clients who come to me with completely closed throat chakras, insecurities, low confidence, self-doubt, limiting beliefs, fear of self-assertiveness, etc., due to psychological and emotional traumas, and childhood conditioning.

In retrospect, the first time I intentionally used my voice therapeutically was when I started mowing lawns for extra money when I was a young teenager, although I really didn't understand what I was doing at the time. Instead of using earplugs or listening to music in headphones, I hummed with the lawnmower motor. I would *listen* and *feel* the vibrations and harmonize with its dominant drone frequency. Having the language to describe it now, I was constructing a coherent resonant sonic field out of otherwise destructive noise, one that my body could easily assimilate. I did this naturally and intuitively, much like the day I was born, I imagine.

My experience was that I could not only tolerate the loud sound of the lawnmower, but I was also moved into a trance state of vibrational alignment with the sound and was able to mow large lawns in a meditative state and feel rejuvenated and energized afterward.

Today I don't have a lawn to mow. Instead, I harmonize in this way with my vacuum cleaner, my high-powered blender, and my favorite, my electric toothbrush. Humming a pitch that's in harmony with the strongest frequency of a motor will generate a coherent sonic field that's healthy for your body and energy. This is a secret of humming. Try it at home and write to me of your discoveries. I'd love to hear about them.

Growing up I exhibited a highly developed musical aptitude. I begged my parents to give me piano lessons. It became apparent I was a prodigy. Playing the piano brought me the greatly needed outlet for my complex emotional expression and I was soon to compose original pieces. It also, unfortunately, became a source of intense performance anxiety, pressure, obsession with perfectionism, and rigidity of execution when performing publicly. God forbid I played the wrong note.

The pressure for me to win or place at competitions was nothing compared to the pressure I placed on myself when playing my original music in front of others. I was so hyper-critical of mistakes I'd made, I wasn't able to appreciate the beauty of my own music and performances. Despite my talent, I was a self-incarcerated prisoner to the notes on the page for many years.

One thing to mention, it was at those tedious piano recitals that I first learned to trace my finger around the rim of a water glass to make it hum. This was the tiny seed that would blossom into a profound awakening for me and the liberation from my musical imprisonment to follow.

In addition to music, my development was guided by unusual occurrences.

When I was very young, I had a recurring nightmare where I was being chased by a black puma. Each time, just as I leaped to safety, it slashed my back with its claws and I woke up in pain. I later learned that this is an indication of shamanic initiation. In shamanic traditions, the shaman uses rituals and ceremonies to transform fear.

I believe I faced my first shamanic initiation at the age of 11. I started to feel an invisible presence in my bedroom that terrified me. I wouldn't go upstairs alone. The fear of this unseen presence went on for weeks until one day I was sent to my room. I screamed and shouted for my parents to let me out because I was terrified of the presence in the room with me.

With no other options, I confronted my fear. I turned my back to the door and faced the presence. It immediately entered my solar plexus and I was no longer afraid.

What just happened? I asked myself.

The presence was gone. I never sensed it again. Overnight I became interested in the occult and esoteric studies searching for answers. Within a few years, I was reading Carl Jung. Eventually Dolores Cannon's work on soul integrations provided an explanation.

When I was a freshman in college, I woke one night to find a glowing angel hovering above my bed who proceeded to hand me a flaming sword. I later understood I was given the sword of truth by Archangel Michael. That was the *first* time I was visited by one of the Archangels.

These are a few examples of the many unique experiences including more shamanic initiations, soul integrations, and angelic visitations that helped shape my beliefs and guide me along my path.

But what was I to make of it all?

During my senior year I repeatedly asked myself,

"What's my purpose?"

And I repeatedly got the surprising answer,

"To sing!"

How could that be? I don't sing. What does it mean? Is this metaphorical? This doesn't make any sense to me.

Around the same time, I started hearing a mysterious drone in my head. It sounded unlike any instrument I had ever heard. I was compelled to sing and harmonize with it in the shower. It was so alluring, I even composed a chamber piece for my senior thesis with a passage inspired by it. I orchestrated for the tones produced by circling around the rims of wine glasses because that was the closest sound to what I heard in my head. Little did I know I was experiencing clairaudiently of what I would discover to be the sound of quartz crystal singing bowls.

From shamanic initiations, to angelic visitations, to my cryptic purpose, and mysterious sounds in my head, I was being shown the way.

Each year, two graduating music majors are awarded a fellowship to stay on as either the assistant orchestral director, or assistant choral director. Having a background in piano, percussion, and cello, I naturally applied for the orchestral assistant. To my surprise, I was offered the choral assistant position!

Suddenly the message "to sing" made a whole lot of sense.

I said "Yes!" to the opportunity.

With no experience, I found myself directing four choral groups and singing in three of them. Talk about an initiation! I also received a year of formal classical voice training. Interestingly, that teacher handed me a copy of Barbara Brennan's seminal work on energy healing, *Hands of Light,* out of the blue at our last lesson saying,

"I think this will come in handy for you in the future."

Receiving that book partially influenced my decision to attend school for massage therapy after completing my fellowship at Amherst College. That decision set in motion a series of probabilities that ultimately led me to enroll in a sound healing institute where I first encountered a quartz crystal singing bowl.

I can best describe the sensation as an opening, like someone unlocked a hatchway in my head, and said, "Welcome home."

This is the sound that has been haunting me for four years!

Within two weeks, I manifested my own quartz singing bowl. My first instinct was to hum with it. When humming, my whole chest cavity would vibrate. I observed how when I hummed the exact same pitch, the physical vibrations inside me would intensify. The secrets of humming once again began to reveal themselves to me.

Not limited to humming, I began to vocalize, to *'tone'* with the bowl. I became fascinated by the correlation of bodily sensations produced by the interaction of the sounds of my voice in relation to the pitch of the bowl. Through experimentation and exploration, I developed an entire realm of expression and discovery within the boundaries of my breath and body.

I found that uninterrupted toning for extended periods of time brought me to heightened states of consciousness, deep states of bliss, emotional release, healing, and inner peace. I developed self-mastery and incredible body awareness through the use of my breath and voice. To this day, I employ this simple life-management skill almost every day to clear my mind, emotions, and field to stay balanced and aligned.

Singing with crystal bowls emancipated me from the learned restrictions that rigid classical musical training had imposed upon me. I was at last, liberated in my expression! What's best—no stage fright! It helped me overcome performance anxiety when playing piano publicly as well. All of those earlier experiences in my life were contextualized and their meanings became clear to me, and I had healed the trauma.

Toning also helped me to discover other gifts. While toning, I received the next pitch in my head and learned to sing channeled songs and chants. I started holding sound healing meditations and doing this in front of other people with amazing results!

It wasn't until I gave myself permission to fully express myself in public that the true magic of healing began manifesting amidst my audiences.

I could call in angels and indigenous spirits. I soon opened to channel them directly through my voice. I'd unlocked the secret of humming and self-actualized as a shamanic angelic sound healer.

The seeds of my healing transformation through self-discovery were planted in my first performance as that miraculous humming baby. Perhaps I wanted to remind myself and others of the one tool we all carry within us, our voices, and how simple it is to use.

Rediscovering the true power of my voice helped free me from limitations and restrictions in my personal life and career. Now I offer clients techniques for personal transformation using their voices as well. Allow me to share the secret of humming with you.

The Medicine

Here are a few simple exercises for you to begin using your voice as a tool for managing stress and clearing stuck emotions. Try not to let self-criticism and self-consciousness prevent you from fully exploring the sound of your own voice.

Find a private place where you can feel comfortable making sounds.

Inhale deeply, then audibly sigh on your entire exhale. Pay attention to the vibrations in your body. Repeat this seven times.

Pause. Notice how you feel.

Now inhale, then hum a pitch for the entire exhale. Place your hand on your chest to better feel the vibrations. Hum seven times exploring different pitches. Notice how different places inside you vibrate.

Pause. Notice how you feel.

Humming simulates the sensation of being in the womb. It's nurturing, calming, reduces anxiety, brings you back into your body, and grounds you.

Now you're ready to begin toning.

On the next exhale produce and sustain the vowel sound "Oh" until the end of your breath. Inhale slowly and completely and immediately exhale "Oh" again, six more times consecutively without interruption. Tone the same pitch each time.

Notice how you feel.

This opens and expands your energy while clearing stress and releasing blocked emotions. It's that simple.

Now do the same seven times with the vowel sound "Ah." This is a heart opener and can lift your mood and raise your energy.

Next alternate humming "Oh" and "Ah" multiple times within a single breath. Do this three times. Focus on the changing inner sensations. Notice how much longer your exhale lasts.

Lastly, tone A-U-M (Ohm) seven times, slowly transitioning between the vowels, closing on "M" as a hum. You're now embodying the sacred Sanskrit seed syllable for all creation, opening your heart, expanding your energy, and grounding within.

Notice how you feel.

Visit www.BradfordTilden.com to download a free toning track where you can practice the above exercises with me.

Bradford W. Tilden MM, CMT, UWT is a best-selling author, internationally recognized composer, pianist, sound healer, and leading teacher of Universal White Time Healing in the United States. He graduated *magna cum laude* from Amherst College in 2002, received a master's in music composition from UMASS, Amherst, in 2014, and is a graduate of the Globe Institute of Sound and Consciousness in San Francisco, California. He is also an initiate of the Puma tribe of the Q'ero shamans of Peru.

Bradford is the founder of the Lemurian School of Intuitive Natural Healing. The mission of LSINH, (pronounced "listen") is to develop one's intuition while opening up to the power of vocal sound and crystals to become an effective healer for oneself and the world. It is derived from the knowledge of the ancient Lemurian civilization, as revealed to him by his UWT master guides and Lemurian priest-healers through his work with Lemurian seed crystals.

Bradford channels angelic and shamanic healing frequencies with his voice. His musical compositions and live sound journeys are divinely orchestrated collaborations with higher beings. His Archangel Meditations combine channeled music with gemstone layouts. He also composes for MediMind, a guided meditation app. Find his music at https://bradfordwtilden.bandcamp.com

Bradford helps people who feel lost, disconnected, and unfulfilled to reconnect with their divine essence and life purpose. He offers in-person and remote sessions incorporating sound, UWT gemstone and energy healing, spiritual guidance, and transformational vocal coaching. He's available for group sound journeys, performances, commissions, interviews, and presentations. He will travel anywhere in the world to teach. Contact him to host a class in your local community.

Visit www.CrystalMusicHealing.com to learn more about Bradford and UWT. Visit https://linktr.ee/bradfordtilden for access to his social media, articles, and more. Reach him at Bradford@CrystalMusicHealing.com

"Rediscovering the true power of my voice helped free me from limitation and restriction in my personal life and career."

~ Bradford W. Tilden

CHAPTER 9

HERE ARE YOUR WINGS, DO YOUR THING

TURNING ANCESTRAL GUIDANCE INTO INSPIRED ACTION

Suzanne Rollen

My Story

The woman in the mirror stared back at me, anguish filling her eyes, as I read the engraved message on the mirror, "You are beautiful."

No. I'm not. Not anymore.

A single lock of hair remained on my head. I twirled it around my finger, gripping, holding back tears—that's what I knew.

At least I'm strong. I'm still strong, right?

I placed my new wig on my bare head, hoping it would restore faith, and returned my gaze to the mirror.

Who are you? Do I even know you? You're not me.

"Aaaghhh!"

I grasped the wig, ripping it from my head. My refusal to cry meant nothing to the tears welling in my eyes. Red-faced, chin quivering, I collapsed to the floor.

One hand burying my face in the wig, the other palming my scalp, I surrendered the fight.

No. Not even strong. I'm broken.

I see now how out of balance my life was, but I had no concept of balance. I knew no other way. I was an overachiever and perfectionist. I did everything for everyone.

I couldn't stop. If I stopped, I'd feel. If I felt, they'd know I was a mess and I wouldn't be enough.

When I wasn't at work, I was at the doctor's office. My life was a constant battle to find the right prescription to quell the side effects of the other medications I was taking for a laundry list of ailments.

I had to keep the chronic migraines in check to make it through another 18-hour day at the tech job I hated. I mean, of course, I did, right? How else could I prove my worth?

I'm in a man's world. I have to keep up.

Although there were days I couldn't work through the excruciating pain, get my eyes to focus on the computer screen, or even unscramble my brain enough to think, I tried to hide the debilitating impact of my migraines.

I had long, thick hair. One evening, I noticed a small patch missing, then another. Soon, chunks would fall out in my hands as I shampooed or brushed. I parted it differently and tried dark sprays and bandanas, desperate to conceal this crack in my façade.

Alopecia not only stole my hair and my ability to hide. It was suddenly obvious that I wasn't okay.

In that moment of grief on the floor, I felt defeated and alone. I'd stacked the bricks of my tough exterior too high to see those who were there to support me.

The myriad of health issues that impacted my ability to function physically and mentally didn't provide enough motivation to change.

Alopecia, the one that caused no physical pain or disability, was the chink in my armor, catalyst, and ultimately one of the biggest gifts of my life.

Over time, I found ways to slow down and reclaim my heart. Flying trapeze classes renewed a spark of joy. Acupuncture and yoga brought peace, gentle movement, and reminders to honor my body.

I recognized I was hanging on to my job out of obligation and a fear of losing my health insurance.

How will I afford all these doctors and treatments?

As my desire for more time to enjoy a healthier lifestyle grew, my disdain for my job did, too. It was time.

Everything I'm doing is working. I'm healing. I'm safe to let go.

I found a part-time online job and took a leap of faith. Sure enough, I was fine and began thriving. I no longer needed the doctors and pharmaceuticals.

For the first time in decades, I began to enjoy life.

As my energy returned, I revived an old career goal. I took a part-time job as a Speech-Language Pathology Assistant and jumped into grad school, research projects, and clinicals. My schedule filled and I had less and less time for all of the practices that nourished my body and spirit.

I reverted to old patterns. Without a thought, I heaved that familiar-feeling boulder of obligation, perfectionism, and achievement back onto my shoulders.

My saving grace was that I listened to inspirational audiobooks during my commute and was planting seeds for a different way of thinking and being.

However, it was too late to save my marriage from the pressure that had built up. Before those seeds could sprout, everything collapsed around me.

My husband and I were both buried under the weight of all we'd been carrying. We desperately tried to save each other and the whole world, without knowing how to look at ourselves.

It was finals week. Projects due, exams looming, work and clinicals weighing on me, and my marriage was in shambles.

Migraines returned and my body felt weak. My solar plexus trembled, my jaw clenched, and I couldn't hold anymore.

Why am I trading my life, my soul for straight As? And why do As feel like a failure?

My mind swam with overwhelm, sorrow, anger, and what-ifs.

I suck. Even doing things 'right' doesn't feel right.

Exasperated, my hands grasped my scalp with a smack, and I laid my head on my desk, gripping everything I had left.

I gotta finish this paper. Focus, brain. Focus!

I can't.

I had a sudden flash of an invitation I saw for a global prayer of peace for the Water Protectors and our Mother Earth. It echoed in my thoughts like it was calling to me.

Ugh. I'd love that, but I don't have time.

The uneasy sensation in my solar plexus dissipated. I felt a pull, a tingle, almost like butterflies.

But, I'm supposed to?

Another flitter in my abdomen.

My body is saying, "Yes!"

It was a clear yes!

What is this? I paused to feel.

I wasn't used to listening to my body, or even noticing it, for that matter. I was logical, an intellectual. Things needed to make sense.

My ego tried to convince me I was nuts and that I should just return to my cozy little home in my brain.

Thankfully, a wise inner voice spoke.

How's that working for you? Don't you think it's time to try something different?

In that instant, I relinquished the false sense of control I held fast to, and chose my intuition. I chose myself.

I'm done.

That single hour I took for myself changed the course of my life. I prayed for peace, the people, the water, and the land. I prayed for myself.

Energy built within me; a spark ignited. All I had to do to save myself was stop fighting. It was time to be still, listen, allow, and trust. There was something bigger holding me, guiding me. I was stepping into faith.

I realized that grad school and my career path were just my latest attempts to do what I thought I was supposed to.

I accepted that my marriage was no longer healthy for either of us.

I let go.

Over the next few years, I became a seeker. I went to counseling, retreats, and women's circles. I connected to God, my guides, and ancestors through shamanic journeying and breathwork.

I played, hiked, drummed, traveled, and opened my heart. I learned to trust again. I found people who inspire and encourage me, and communities to nurture me through any challenges.

I faced old traumas, forgave others, danced with my shadows, forgave myself, and released destructive patterns.

I found divine feminine flow. After a lifetime of doing, achieving, pushing, and competing, I softened and learned to receive.

I began drawing, painting, meditating, journaling, gardening, climbing trees, and talking to birds. I started cooking real food to nourish my body and feel my best.

Life became magical, whimsical, and full of richness, love, gratitude, and light.

I remembered my wholeness, health, and joy. My ability to trust, accept what is, and honor myself has allowed me to hold on to these, even as my path led me to be a caregiver for multiple family members.

This reconnection to my divine feminine allowed me to nurture my dad in his final months with dementia and Parkinson's, and my aunt, as she prepares to transition.

I learned tools and practices to ground myself, recenter, endure, and even value the darkest days, because they're among my greatest teachers.

There is a flip side. I've struggled to find direction, though I know there is something bigger waiting for me.

I shy away from commitments because of past experiences with burnout, when I didn't have the self-worth or healthy boundaries to use my sacred "no."

I find myself in another time of transition, being called to find my own balance of sacred masculine and divine feminine. That means I get to relearn the masculine side with a new, healthier understanding.

As a caregiver, I've developed a deep connection to my ancestors. Through them, I've gained confidence, inspiration, clarity, guidance, protection, healing, and a greater understanding of the gifts I carry.

My grandmother, known to me as Narnee, was no delicate southern belle. She was tough, forged by the unforgiving labor of farm life in rural Alabama. Narnee was resilient, with an understated fierceness. She just did what she had to do.

She came of age in the Great Depression. Times were tough and there were a lot of expectations about how young women should act in their humble, Baptist homes and community.

Practicality was not only the way of life, but a matter of survival. Creativity took a backseat.

Life all changed when Narnee married Pawpaw. Military orders sent them to San Diego, a world away from family and the country life she was accustomed to.

When he was sent to the Pacific as a Marine Captain in World War II, she became a real-life Rosie the Riveter.

Far from home, suddenly on her own, and still grieving the loss of their first infant son, writing became her steadfast companion. Throughout WWII, their only form of communication was handwritten letters.

Pawpaw adored Narnee and was inspired and charmed by her writing abilities. For the first time, and perhaps the only time, she felt safe to let someone into her heart and mind.

Once they returned to Alabama to raise their children, she put her writing aside. Her tidy home, southern cooking, handmade clothing, embroidered linens, and her award-winning flower garden, became her canvas. The kids grew and moved on.

Like a thief in the night, devastation arrived, stealing my grandfather, and gripping my grandmother. His sudden and unexpected cardiac arrest shattered her.

In the following years, as her sight began to fail, she moved in with my aunt. As she let go of her home of nearly 30 years, and grappled with how to process her deep, unending grief, she pulled out her old box of letters and journals.

It was too much, too vulnerable. The safety Narnee found in the intimate exchanges with her sweetheart was gone. She crumpled page after page and lit a match.

Smoke swirled as she held in her tears. Ever the stoic, she didn't even know how to let them escape when she was alone with the crackle of flames. She surrendered every letter, every story she'd jotted down, every single doodle and idea, praying her heartache would float away with the ashes.

While on a retreat, I was invited to participate in a standing breathwork ceremony, which elicited a state similar to that of lucid dreaming.

Blackness.

The music started. Badum bum. . .badum bum. . .

They seriously expect me to dance, to take a step? I don't know where I am, much less where I'm going. I can't do this!

Badum bum. . .badum bum. . .

I staggered and caught myself.

Can I do this?

The beat surged up my spine, dispersing the slumber I carried across the courtyard from my bed.

It's too early, my sleep-deprived body screamed, as I attempted to steady my long, wobbly legs.

Blindfolded, bundled in a baja hoodie, sherpa hat, and wrapped in a woven blanket, I took a deep breath, and another.

Why am I doing this? My teeth chattered, as I pulled the cold air deep into my lungs and blew it out again.

I'm doing this.

I stumbled again, regaining my footing.

I need to root, to find my balance. Narnee, I need your grounding.

She has shown up for me as rock formations, steppingstones, and earth, guiding my way, supporting me, and nurturing me. I planted my feet until I found the rhythm.

Pawpaw, my eagle guide, I need your sight.

Each time I got too close to another person, a facilitator would gently guide me to safety.

See, I'm safe, I reminded myself. *This is a perfect metaphor!*

As I gained confidence, my body moved more fluidly to the beat.

I turned my body and, in the blackness, I began to see shapes. The Pyramid of the Moon rose from the ground. We'd just visited the pyramids of Teotihuacán, Mexico, the day before, so they were fresh in my mind's eye.

I envisioned the base of the pyramid as a womb space, amid the earthen stones, gestating a ball of creative energy and light. I traced my eyes upward to see the glow of a nearly full moon radiating her love down on me and the earth below my feet.

Pawpaw, circling as an eagle, guided my eyes with his majestic wings. The Pyramid of the Sun rose behind me. I allowed my body to turn to the beat of the pulsating music.

A full-maned lion, the ultimate protector and symbol of balance, sat regally at the base of the pyramid.

I saw a giant infinity symbol and began sweeping my arms to trace it. Divine feminine intuition and guidance to the left, sacred masculine safety and protection to the right. Back to the left, into the flow and nurturing energy, then to the right into structure and action.

Just like I found my balance in this dance in the darkness, feet rooted on both sides, I was being asked to reclaim balance in my life by integrating my natural masculine and feminine energies.

I get it. I am safe to pause and listen to my intuition. I can act with confidence because I know I'm divinely inspired.

Pawpaw nodded as he flew over me.

I cherish every word Narnee wrote, but she was afraid. You carry her gift for writing, and you are meant to bring light to the world.

He descended over me, placing giant wings over my shoulders.

You are safe. Open your wings. It's time for you to soar.

Our personal masculine/feminine balance is rarely 50/50. We each have a place on the spectrum that feels more natural. I also believe that this changes throughout life, from day to day, depending on the situation, the people we're with, and our personal needs and desires.

It's a beautiful dance of divine energies.

Since my breathwork experience, I have found a new sense of security, knowing I can trust my guidance and step confidently into new opportunities to share my light. It doesn't mean my fears are gone, but my faith in myself and others has grown.

I feel healthier with more flow in my day. However, I recognize that having some guardrails in place reminds me I'm safe to be me and take inspired action.

The Medicine

Connecting with my ancestors, especially my dad and grandparents, has become a part of my day. I share my heart, laugh, cry, and ask for support. I feel their love and guidance through signs, intuition, journaling, and automatic writing.

When I'm feeling stuck, uninspired, afraid, or confused, I write a letter to an ancestor.

I invite you to write a letter to one of your ancestors and practice receiving a response through automatic writing.

Take a moment to set your intention and sacred space.

- How do you need to be supported right now?
- Is there an ancestor who carries the gifts and wisdom that you seek?
  - I call on Narnee for creative inspiration, to be nurtured, for guidance in caregiving, or to ground. I call on Pawpaw for courage, protection, perspective shifts, faith in the big picture, and remembering my worth.
  - If you don't know your ancestors or don't feel safe with the ones you know, write to unknown ancestors. They're available and ready to support you.

- If you have special items that belonged to your ancestors or remind you of them, place them near you or even hold them as you write. Some of my favorites are the wings my dad earned as a Navy pilot, a necklace, Pawpaw's deputy badge, and a rock from Zimbabwe that represents Narnee.
- Consider lighting a candle or burning incense.
- Settle in, breathe deeply, and picture them in your mind.
  - No matter what they were like in life, see them in their highest form, healed, and whole.

- Begin writing your letter from your heart. Be completely open and honest. Just let it flow.
- Once your letter feels complete, try automatic writing to receive a response.
  - This moves us out of our busy minds and to a more open, receptive state.
  - I recommend using your non-dominant hand. Trust what comes through for you, don't edit, just flow. Allow your handwriting to be messy. It's about the messages received, not how it looks.
  - (I'm right-handed, so switching to my left hand allows me to activate the right hemisphere, which is more creative and attuned to intuition and emotion.)

When you're done, offer gratitude to your ancestors and be gentle with yourself. You may find that messages can come through for several days.

Return to this practice as often as you feel a need for support, connection, and guidance. Love and wisdom are always available from our ancestors, without conditions or limits. Enjoy your experience with them. May it bring you peace, balance, and new perspective.

Suzanne Rollen is known for her curious mind, joyful spirit, and compassionate heart.

She ditched corporate life over a decade ago, to restore her physical and mental health. The flexibility of an online job has allowed her the time and space to remember herself and find the balance she so desperately needed.

She's discovered that true balance comes through a deep spiritual connection, having the courage to change and release what doesn't work, and finding things that spark the fire in her heart.

She's passionate about travel and celebrates the richness of the world around her. She's fascinated by the diversity of cultures and inspired by people who carry ancient wisdom and have a deep connection to the land.

She's followed her heart to the pyramids of Teotihuacán, Mexico, the sacred lands of Zimbabwe, and the magnificent white lions of South Africa. Her adventurous soul has led her to flying trapeze, firewalking, and zip-lining through the rainforest in Costa Rica.

Her creativity flows through painting, drawing, photography, and writing.

She seeks solace in nature and cherishes moments by a creek, under a tree, or even up a tree. While hiking with Peanut, her magical mutt, you're likely to hear her talking to birds, squirrels, bugs, and plants, as she makes friends everywhere and sees beauty in all things.

As she wanders through the world, she is honored to be of service to others. Her big heart led her to volunteer with wildlife, sit with elders in hospice care, and remind kids with special needs and foster kids that they have a special purpose in life.

For nearly three years, she's lovingly taken on the role of caregiver for multiple members of her family.

She's so grateful for the gifts life brings her each and every day.

Connect with Suzanne at:
Facebook https://www.facebook.com/Author.SuzanneRollen

"Just like I found my balance in this dance in darkness, feet rooted on both sides, I was being asked to reclaim balance in my life by integrating my natural masculine and feminine energies."

~ Suzanne Rollen

CHAPTER 10

ARTISTIC ALCHEMY

PAINTING THE CANVAS OF SELF WITH LIFE'S PALLET

Kya Dubois

My Story

"This is a joke, right?" a note of plea was in my voice. "They're just late picking me up, I'm sure."

I felt the words fall off my lips, seemingly at the speed of light in contrast to the room around me, suddenly stuck in slow motion. I knew the words weren't true, but I let them fall anyway.

My eyes darted between the faces of sympathy around me. An anxious chuckle escaped the bewilderment and shock plastered across my face. The up-turned corners of my mouth could almost be mistaken for a smile.

Two weeks shy of my eighteenth birthday and two months close to graduation, I found myself in the small, unbecoming conference room of the basement of my employment—a diner-style chain restaurant confused about its identity of Ukrainian or mid-western cooking. Either way, you could call it traditional I suppose. Traditional, like the uninspiring conservative town my parents dragged me to five years prior.

The officer in front of me stood awkwardly in his duty, the necessary stoic nature of his job at odds with the fatherly energy of a middle-aged man wishing to console the suddenly orphaned adolescent girl in front of him.

Between heavy and faltered breaths I took in the unremarkable room surrounding me.

How incredibly fitting. An unremarkable room, in a space that doesn't support me, within an equally unremarkable town that doesn't support me.

What a setting; what a scene for such a truly remarkable moment.

The irony. Hilarious. Thanks, Mom

A sarcastic laugh slipped out.

Five years can feel like a lifetime to a teenager, but it's gone in a flash. I never truly found my place in those five years. There was a void where my artistic community should be and I resented my parents for it. Abruptly pulled up from my roots in pottery class, drawing 101, dance studio, circus camp, and a respectively funded education system, I found myself thrown into some slow-paced, mountain town I had never heard of.

A child of nature (born on Earth Day don't you know?) I quickly came to love the landscape around me; the expansive, unpolluted sky above me and towering, awesome mountain ranges cradled the small city on every side. In this aspect, I quickly came home to gratitude.

But with all this space to grow my branches skyward, I had nowhere to place my roots. Unable to bury into nourishing soil, my roots began to starve and thirst until they shriveled into stillness—calcified.

Petrified wood sure is something beautiful to look at, a pretty shiny gem in your hand. Its rings and grooves, a moment frozen in time forever. But something petrified no longer lives. Something frozen does not grow. And that's what I had become—petrified wood.

I never knew my father, abandoned by him (albeit, unbeknownst to him). My beautiful mother, as hard as she loved me, emotionally abandoned me as I came of age. When my stepfather arrived in the picture, that space between us deepened with a lack of communication. Then came the final and permanent abandonment: death. And so I gave in to the pattern I came to know. I abandoned myself.

Why should I remain when no one else has stayed?

I committed a spiritual suicide of sorts. I severed the authentic pieces of myself, lopping off each decaying, dead branch long deprived of nourishment. I took my own life; the conscious, present me no longer remained.

As the lifeless, petrified wood that I was, there was nothing to live for. I made reckless and careless decisions, with no regard for my well-being or those around me. I poisoned my mind and body with alcohol, leaning too far into the 'life of the party' persona. So far, in fact, I became the nuisance and heavy baggage of the party—out of control, malicious, and defiant, not anyone's favorite party guest. I poisoned my spirit and sacral with un-empowering, blurry, and forgetful sex. I surrounded myself with an equally poisoned company, while the few who tried to guide me outwards were putting their spiritual and physical lines in danger.

I continually hurt and abandoned myself every day. And in doing so, I hurt and abandoned those around me. I did anything that spiked some adrenaline, a false sense of life within me, not knowing what I truly craved was real-life essence.

I tried on every mask but my own, danced every step designed for others' feet, and tapped the sap from others' flourishing trees.

I bounced from one abusive relationship to another, tasting all the flavors until I landed in the most violent of its forms. A small inner voice emerged, having my life threatened at the hands of another instead of my own.

I don't want this. I want to live.

Within that space, a seed sprouted. And as these new roots found their way into my limbs, they guided my hands back into art.

I surrendered to the process.

I realized that while I had ceased to exist, my earthly avatar had not. It, too, had been abandoned and neglected, a forgotten canvas collecting dust in the corner of a dark closet.

As I came back to life, my avatar fell out of alignment. This canvas no longer matched my inner vision and I had grown tired of keeping my vision tucked away in sacred keeping.

So I painted.

Life was the canvas and I, the prolific artist. Looking too closely at my canvas, I could only see each imperfection, small cracks, and unblended color. I couldn't see the forest through the trees.

But when I took a step back, oh! What a masterpiece!

I no longer saw the grief held deeply within me as a heavy weight to be shed. What I saw were beautiful under-paintings primed for the next evolution, stark contrasts that brought more vibrancy to the whole picture, and deep rigid textures to dance my brushes over.

Blended mediums coming and going between each other were a delight for my eyes to behold. Combative styles having no business being next to each other intertwined in a sexual dance giving birth to beautiful new beings, the likes of which I had never seen before.

Life became an ecstatic, sensual banquet because I made it so. The colors were more vibrant, the food more decadent, and the air sweeter. Because that's the masterpiece I saw myself living.

The more I painted my outer world with my authentic self, the stronger my roots became. The stronger my roots became, the longer my branches grew. The longer my branches grew, the more colorful the fruits that hung. And when those fruits ripened they fell to the ground, exploding in a shower of paint, turning everything in that splash zone into a vibrant rainbow. What I saw is that the more I lived uninhibited, artfully, and vibrantly out loud, the more it gave permission for the souls and world around me to follow suit. Painted ripples flowed freely in every direction.

I fell in love with life again when I took control of my canvas. I took ownership of my colors, how I used them, where I placed them, and what I created with them.

You are the canvas. Each moment, a brush stroke. Each thought, a new color. Each breath, a new tool.

Life is your masterpiece.

Go ahead, put a happy little tree in it.

Really, Bob Ross that shit up.

The Medicine

We are our most important canvas, the never finished, always-in-progress, endlessly fine-tuned, ever-critiqued canvas.

We are the canvas that never ends, an ever-shifting style, layer upon layer upon layer until eventually, these many layers peel away under the weight of themselves, and the cycle starts anew.

Artists may paint the world around them, their inner world and the metaphors they speak in. They may participate in and curate galleries—galleries collaborated through aesthetics, aligned philosophies, and mirrored themes.

But what is truly happening is a public spectacle of self-proclamation, a cry into the megaphone for healing's sake, a free and global gallery of each intimate moment, traumatic event, and self-contained enlightenment.

The artist's life is a gallery, hall after hall after hall, with spacious hanging, maximalist chaos, and nuanced lighting, intrinsically curated to appear both intimate and aloof.

So, how do you start painting?

First, I want you to throw out everything you think you know or believe to be 'art.' No limiting beliefs on your perceived artistic talent or lack thereof.

I don't care if you can't draw a stick man to save your life; every single one of us is an artist. We all house the Divine power of creation and the ability to birth new life in so many diverse forms.

And while I believe that every one of us has the potential to learn a material, physically creative skill, for the sake of this exercise, we're moving within the metaphorical cosmos.

EXERCISE #1

Pull out your favorite journal, notepad, or preferred manner of written expression.

Perhaps it's a journal with exquisite cover art that inspires your inner artist.

Next, create your sacred space. Perhaps it's sitting or lying on your bed with the blinds drawn and headphones playing your favorite meditation music. Maybe it's in front of your altar, lighting a candle surrounded by your favorite crystals. Or it could be in your yard or favorite local park with the warm sun on your face, a breeze in your hair and feet in the grass.

Whatever canvas brings you to your most serene, paint yourself into it.

Get comfortable and relax. Take a slow body scan from crown to root, releasing all tension that may be residing. Release your brow, your lips, and your jaw. Drop your shoulders, and unclench your hands. Relax your glutes, let your knees drop, and wiggle your toes until they release.

Take your time.

Take ten deep breaths or as many as you need to come to a meditative center.

Match the counts of your inhales to your exhales.

1, 2, 3, 4, 5. Hold at the top for a second. 5, 4, 3, 2, 1.

Imagine before you a door. As you step through it, you find yourself in a gallery with vaulted white ceilings and sparkling floors. There's artwork on every square inch, truly a maximalist wonder that never seems to end.

As you walk through, you come to one particular wall and notice your name at the top. Perhaps this wall is covered in countless individual canvases of every shape, size, and color one could imagine. Or perhaps it's one very large, unending canvas, blending and mixing more colors than you even knew existed. This is your life's gallery, showcasing every moment, joy, heartache, and triumph you have ever experienced from birth until now.

Visualize tracing your fingers along the nearest section to you. Breathe into your body the textures beneath your fingertips.

Note how the paint feels. Is it dry? Wet? Soft or rigid?

Now take a step back so you can see your entire gallery.

Somewhere within your showcase, you notice a piece that is duller than the rest. What you see is an area in your present life lacking vibrancy.

Focus on it.

What do you see? Take note of what this muted piece is showing you.

Take your time.

When you feel saturated in understanding the message, you may choose to remove this piece from your gallery and take it with you, or you may choose to leave it. Turn back towards the door, leave your gallery and close the door behind you.

Time to come back to the waking world.

Breathe life back into your body. Wiggle your toes, sway your legs, and lighten your breath. Stretch your arms, roll your neck, and gently blink your eyes back to open.

Now take to your journal and write what needs to flow.

Note what part of your life felt dull and lacking vibrancy.

Once you feel fully released onto paper, I want you to break down at least three tangible reasons why this space is so dull.

Then, I want you to write an actionable way to breathe vibrancy into this space pertaining to each reason.

EXAMPLE #1:

Dullness:

My mornings are a muted sepia tone, not quite grey, but monotone and faded in color. I am not a morning person. I hate having to get out of bed when I am comfortable. Mornings are my least favorite part of the day. I move through them on autopilot.

Vibrancy:

I will create a morning space or outfit that is cozy and comfy, making the transition from bed softer and more gradual. I love Sudoku, so I will create an intentional morning activity of drinking my coffee and playing one puzzle as something to look forward to. When stirring my coffee, I recite words of intention for my day into each stir as a small ritual of morning magic.

EXAMPLE #2:

Dullness:

My sex life is monotone grey and un-alive. I'm not as active as I wish to be in my sex life. I'm losing touch with my sexuality and sensuality. My sex life is not as interesting, magical, or tantric as I would like it to be.

Vibrancy:

While I cannot make others active participants in my sex life, I can be my most active partner. I will treat myself to a new crystal pleasure wand, carnelian to tap into my sensual sacral. I will paint a self-love ritual each week, in which I wear my most empowering outfit, light candles, dance to tantric beats to build energy, and end with a self-pleasure session in front of the mirror.

This first exercise is a longer meditation and great practice for a deeper dive into the areas of your life lacking vibrancy and color. It's a versatile exercise that can be breathed into any aspect of your life.

EXERCISE #2

This is a shorter practice, intended as a morning meditation to breathe vibrancy into the rest of your day.

Find a comfortable, quiet spot and create your sacred space. Relax. Softly close your eyes. Take a slow body scan from crown to root, releasing all tension that may be residing.

Start to deepen your breath. Be in control, mindful and present.

Begin to visualize your roots reaching down, down into the Earth. They get deeper and deeper as they move their way through the Earth. Down, down they go, becoming stronger, reaching far and wide. Soon you find yourself at the Earth's core. You see that this core is a beautiful, luminous ball of light. Within it contains every color of the rainbow. It glitters and shines like stained glass.

Connect your roots to this ball of light. Now visualize your roots drawing energy from this light. This energy is the consistency of paint, thick and viscous. Your roots joyfully gurgle and slurp up their nourishment.

Watch this energetic paint transferring from the core, through the roots, up, up, up, and into you with each breath. Breathe in this paint, exhale to empty. See every color tinting your veins, your being.

Once you feel saturated, call your roots back to you. Back through every layer of Earth, from every direction, until at last, you feel your roots fully come back to you.

Express gratitude for the Earth in sharing this vibrancy with you.

Set the intention to live your day in full spectrum color.

Lighten your breath.

Gently blink your eyes open.

Step into your day with vibrancy.

To live your life artfully and to become an artistic alchemist, is to recognize your life as the masterpiece it is. The artistic alchemist can see every brushstroke across the timeline—this and all timelines. They are multi-dimensional tool bearers, fluidly shifting from painting to sculpting, sketching to inking, engaging every medium at their disposal to create their reality and the reality around them. When you live in an example, lead with vibrancy, so does the world follow suit.

So I leave you with this spell:

Art is power

Art is freedom

I do not know of any individual more powerful than the Artist; being able to bend things most people see as a straight line.

Art is that bridge over tension between the internal and external worlds

Art is alchemy

The transmutation of vibrations, thoughts, trauma, love, wisdom

Art is the trifecta where hands, heart, and mind become one.

Art is activism

It's political, it's spiritual, it's multi-dimensional

The Artist is immortal, living forever through their art and the souls they touched, the seeds they plant

The Artist dives deep into the Sacred, tapping into the power of birth, creating and molding new worlds, new life, and vibrational offspring

The Artist may seek accolades or may keep their expressions held close to their heart; neither more valid than the other

The Artist

The most powerful teacher, healer and multi-dimensional Being

Kya Dubois is a visionary artist and creatrix, relating to the world through visual and audible artworks. As a ten-year tattooist bringing the sacred back into this ancient art, a sculptor merging the worlds of crystals and clay, and a prolific visionary painter, Kya embodies the self-proclaimed title of 'Multi-Dimensional Artist.'

Kya's daily mission is to connect folks to their inner artist, inner Goddess, and most authentic self. She believes in the immense power of authentic vulnerability, regularly sharing her literary spells and raw wordsmithing in the online space. In doing so, she hopes to normalize the complex nuances that make us human, in that the human experience is never linear.

Having reached her branches out further than the art space, Kya is an initiated Wildwood Priestess through The Wildwood Witch School under the mentorship of the prolific and internationally recognized teacher, Dawn Dancing Otter. Kya has also stepped into a plant medicine ceremonial facilitator apprenticeship under the same mentorship. Kya has also studied both under Angel Rohrer's Nina Songo Energy Medicine School, as well as alongside her in kinship for ten years.

In her downtime, well, Kya never really goes 'down.' Every space in her world is filled with art. When she is not bringing forth her client's tattoo visions, Kya works on her latest painting, sculpture, blog post, poem, essay, or music. Art is breathing for Kya, and she might just explode if she holds it in too long! However, she can also be found hiking to the top of mountains, paddle boarding glacier lakes, or satisfying her wanderlust with her latest international adventure.

Connect with Kya:

Facebook: https://www.facebook.com/kyaduboisartist

Instagram: https://www.instagram.com/art.of.kya

Website: https://www.souloftheboreal.ca

TikTok: @kyajdubois

Youtube: Artistic Alchemy Pod

"Life is the canvas and You, the Artist.
You are Art in motion. Create a Masterpiece"

~ Kya Dubois

CHAPTER 11

PLEA OF THE WARRIORESS TO RETURN TO THE SACRED HEART

HOW TO TURN SELF-SABOTAGE INTO SELF-MASTERY

Grace Solaris

My Story

As I stood gazing into the endless tapestry of the starry night, I wondered:

Which one is it?
Could it be that one, so bright and twinkling?

The yearning was piercing through my heart, and it would not let go until I found the answer. A seeking and calling that would become louder and louder. I knew for sure, I wasn't of this crude and cold world. Deep within my heart, I knew I came here to make a difference.

My heart trembled, as I felt the sword of my father's raging voice cutting through the air. The Earth was shivering, as was every cell in my body. Terror pulsated through my skin and my heart throbbed in my throat, as I ran down the hallway. I made it just in time and was able to turn the lock before his hand could grab me. Had I not made it, the outcome would have been a furious spanking!

None of it made sense.

What had I done? What was it in me that ignited the anger in his heart?

I had become his favorite prey and target to release the unresolved anger of his inner child.

This was a scene playing itself out repeatedly throughout my childhood. I felt unsafe, guilty, and shameful. I would rather hide from the world and so I dimmed my light and at times, I hid in the closet for hours crying my heart out.

I became an outcast, but the child within didn't understand, because in my heart I knew I was here for love, to shine light and love into the world.

My mother was absent in her depression. I sensed she was entrapped, hiding inside a void of hopelessness. I sensed a wall of protection keeping me from reaching into her heart. No hope. I was on my own. So, I decided I had to take things into my own hands.

The warrioress within came to my rescue, but my inner child was broken and tormented by the echo of the roaring thunder of my dad's voice.

"How could you, you naughty girl? I'm going to teach you a lesson."

As a teen, an ever-returning thought repeated itself inside my mind:

If I can't do that, I might as well pack my suitcase and leave the planet.

Deep within my heart, I knew I came to heal the world and restore harmony. But I also knew what I was called to do wouldn't happen overnight. My heart was impatient.

The yearning to get on with my mission to bring love and healing was like an arrow piercing deeper and deeper into my heart.

Do not forget; keep going; your time will come.

I became a rebel; I wasn't made to obey. I questioned everything because I couldn't ignore the inner knowing of my heart. I stood up against authority.

Who the fuck are you to tell me what's right and wrong?
Who are you to judge me and belittle me?

So, I set forth my journey to make a change because I knew within my heart, that something wasn't right. But I was tortured by the derogatory loop of thoughts of not being good enough and that something was wrong with me. I started building up walls of protection around me.

The voice of my heart turned increasingly silent.
I became trapped inside my mind.

I knew I had to watch my tongue, but the inner warrioress wouldn't give in.

"You're going to do as I say." A deep-seated rage escaped my dad's ice-blue eyes causing my body to shiver and yet I insisted, "No I'm not." He desperately searched for something to grab and suddenly aimed at me with a coat hanger. His face had morphed into a demon hardly recognizable. I flinched in a split second and avoided the hitting.

The warrioress was not going to allow his physical punishments to continue.

She quickly found balance and took a step towards him. "Don't you dare," the sacred rage of the warrioress caused him to freeze. "No more," she roared.

And yet I was paying less and less attention to the voice of my inner child. She felt alone and defeated. I disconnected from the earth, my body, and my heart to avoid the grief piling up inside me.

I dimmed my light to avoid the broken child in me from being seen.

However, the warrioress was not going to submit.

She wasn't made to be ruled by someone, but to reign from her heart. The voice of my divine feminine, the inner warrioress was fierce and impossible to silence.

You think you are going to break me by hitting and scaring me.

With years of suppression, my dignity and confidence shrank.

Should I just give in?
No way!

She left me no choice but to keep fighting for my freedom and love.

I got up and wiped the tears away, my jaw clenching as I found the strength yet again. She was determined. Nevertheless, my inner child suffered the loss of her innocence by the striking hand of my dad. My heart quivered in my mother's silence and inability to defend me, leaving no space for hope.

The emotional and physical abuse became fuel to my search for God, and so the journey began.

I dove into every religion, belief system, and philosophy I could lay my hands on to find a sense of belonging, from the ancient religions of India to the native mythology and tales of the stars. I signed up for a mystery school, a two-year training, and initiation into the wisdom of ancient Lemuria and Atlantis. My awakening was accelerating; however, again I witnessed how patriarchal dominance gave birth to submission and fake worshipping.

I saw how so many gave their power away to external 'father figures' and abandoned their inner knowing.
One and a half years into the training, my higher self suddenly stepped in and said:

No more.
This has no value to you.
You are giving your power away.
You are not being true to your heart.

I realized what I was taught was just a mind concept, but what my heart was yearning for was a deep heartfelt embodied experience through surrendering to my inner truth. Only by being true to my heart, could I be authentic and love myself. So, I dropped out. I was guided to burn the entire material of one and a half years of training. I burnt every single paper in my stove, one by one, stripping me to the core like an onion, until there was nothing left but an excruciating black void.

This sparked off my dark night of the soul.

I found myself in a void of not knowing. I felt vulnerable and naked to the core. I felt like a failure. This lasted for months, until one day when I felt ready to reconnect with God and open my heart unreserved. I fell on my knees begging God to respond to my longing for home.

"Dear God, I am here before you naked to the core. All I want is to serve you and make a difference in the world." My heart cried out:

"How can I serve you?"

An immense wave of love washed over me permeating every cell of my body and restoring my dignity as I was held in the embrace of God.

I was ready to embark on the journey to unite with the beloved within. I was free of the need for external validation. The stripping of the teaching and beliefs also initiated a stripping of my incarnational story and the identity that played it out to perfection.

I fell apart piece by piece until one night, the last piece, the foundation of the jigsaw, broke apart. I laughed out loud as the realization and remembrance of who I AM came into my awareness, exploding from every cell.

Love is who and what I AM, no more, no less.

All veils lifted in an instant; as I understood, I created it all. I felt uplifted, empowered, and infinite joy filled my entire being as my wings of freedom unfurled. The goddess in me rose in her true glory.

Suddenly it became clear how the patriarchal dominion and agenda, repressing the divine feminine aspect throughout the ages, had played itself out in my personal story.

The goddess in me had a different agenda, refusing to submit to the distortions of patriarchal superiority.

She knew the importance of balancing heart and mind and that this is the key to divine equilibrium and union with God. Through the balancing of the divine feminine and masculine aspects within, the inner beloved is birthed.

The divine feminine and masculine have been fighting an endless battle, creating extreme distortion, power plays, rivalry, and suffering within all humans, and between genders, cultures, and nations, keeping us divided from God.

I realized that all the suffering I went through was the preparation to fulfill my mission of being a midwife for others to unite with God within and live a life of joy.

From there, the eternal love affair with the beloved within began, as my inner divine feminine and masculine united and balance was restored. I learned how to give up control and surrender to the graceful unfolding of life under the heart-aligned leadership of the divine feminine.

I learned that life is effortless and full of grace when we let go and trust in the flow of life. I realized that the more I let go and surrendered to the guidance of the divine feminine force in me, the more life became a dance.

All you need is to be fully grounded in the heart of the present moment—this is the only place where you're aligned and attuned to God. When you get out of your mind into your heart, you're bypassing the interference of ego, which is obsessed with keeping control in its aim to protect you from the suffering of the past.

By being entrapped in the past and in your mind, you're attracting what you're trying to avoid and projecting it into the future. You're living a life in avoidance of what you fear the most.

The nature of the mind is limited by linear thinking and ruled by masculine attributes. It is action oriented and led by logic and reason, whereas the divine feminine is founded in feeling, intuition, and surrender.

Both need to be given space to fulfill their purpose.

However, the divine feminine is the natural principle aligning you with the cosmic flow, which nurtures and keeps you attuned to the truth. She's the seed of all life and the leading principle of creation.

The sacred purpose of the divine masculine is guarding and implementing what she intuits, senses, and receives through deep surrender to God.

Everything in the universe is frequency attracting the corresponding reality.

Every thought, feeling, and act holds a frequency attracting the corresponding external response and manifestation into the physical world. This is the key principle to understanding why situations and specific patterns keep repeating themselves, despite you trying to avoid them. By dwelling in your mind, you're limited by experiences of the past.

To live a life of fulfillment, joy, and abundance, you need to be in a vibrational match with your heart's desire. You need to embody it, smelling, tasting, and feeling it in every cell of your body, as if you already have it. By vibrating it, you're giving it life. It takes conscious intent and deep surrender to allow things to manifest in whatever way serves your highest good.

Surrendering to the inner knowing and intelligence of your heart is living under the guidance and leadership of your divine feminine aspect. It's allowing life to live itself through you without the mind interrupting the natural flow.

So, my love, dare to move beyond fear into the unknown, the unfamiliar, the untried, the outrageous, the juicy stuff making your heart sing with joy, even when your ego screams, "Get me out of here."

It's time to trust your wings.

It's time to soar higher beyond the comfort zone of the known.

This isn't the time for playing it safe; it won't get you where you long to be. It's a time of exploration and discovery of unknown paths—paths no one ever made before you. There are no maps or signs other than following your intuition and inner guidance.

There is no way you are going to figure out where and what to do next.

Plant seeds of intent with your heart here and there and see where energy is flowing and where things are growing. This is where you'll find doors appearing showing you your divine purpose and the steps needed to get there.

It's the doorway to the greatest love story in your life, a safe passageway to home.

The inner beloved will walk beside you, guard you, and guide you.

You do not need to know how, when and what.

Only ego wants to know. And ego wants it complicated.

The path will show itself as you're moving forward with unwavering trust in your heart's inner knowing. All it takes is your uncompromising "yes." You were made to create miracles, make the impossible possible, transcend all limitations, and live an untamed life of passion.

You came here to make a difference and to lead from your heart.

The Medicine

Allow me to introduce you to this healing space, where you can go at any time to receive healing and comfort.

It's the womb of the cosmic mother where you can bring all the lost and fragmented parts of you into wholeness. It's the place where you can receive healing, bring home your inner child, and restore the balance between your divine feminine and masculine. It's a place where you can do forgiveness work and release deep trauma.

It's a place of rebirth, resurrection, and sacred union. Below is a very shortened version and example of a guided meditation on how you can make use of this cave.

So, my love, let me take you by the hand and lead you into this healing space.

First, I'm asking you to take a moment to relax and let go of all control in your body. Still your mind; allow your thoughts to drift by like clouds in the sky and come into the sanctum of your heart.

Now imagine yourself growing solid roots out of your feet down to the center of the Earth, keep going until you cannot get further, and then anchor deep into the core of Mother Earth.

Start breathing in through your nose, deep into the belly and as you exhale let go of all the tension in your body.

Allow yourself to be.

You can be safe here.

You do not need to perform or pretend to be someone different than who you are.

Take a few minutes to breathe deeply into your heart and as you release your breath, let all tension leave your body and empty your mind.

Allow yourself to sink into stillness.

Now imagine yourself entering a cave made of pure rose quartz.

The light is soft and warm and in the middle of the cave, you see a circle of women dressed in long crystalline sparkling robes of light holding hands.

You are urged to step into the middle of the circle.

Now take a few moments to greet each of these beautiful radiant beings, who are smiling at you with such warmth.

You recognize many of the faces and feel overwhelmed by the love emanating from each of them. Each carries a gift of love, a divine virtue of the divine feminine, which is for your healing. One or two might even have a message for you, so listen carefully with your heart.

When you've finished connecting with each of the goddesses, you're ready to call in all aspects of your inner child that have been left in the dark, abandoned, and separated from you. It is time to bring them home. Call from your heart to each of these aspects to come forth and tell them it's time for them to return home and to become whole again.

Now, wait and allow for each of them to show up in their divine timing. One may be reluctant, another may be scared, another timid.

State to your beloved inner child:

I am here with an open heart and open arms to offer you, my love. Know that you are safe, that there's nothing to fear. I'm here for you, so please come closer and let me hold you. Let the tears of feeling unworthy and unlovable leave your heart, know that you matter to me and the world. I see you, beloved child, I see the gift of love in your heart. I love you exactly as you are. Come into my embrace and know you're safe now.

I'm here for you from this moment onwards.

I ask you to please forgive me and trust me. You shall never be abandoned again, never forgotten or forsaken.

I'm committed to guarding you and always love you.

Let go of the shame and guilt, the condemnation and judgment, that has weighed on your heart.

Let go of the burden on your shoulders you have carried for others.

You were meant to shine beloved child. Remember who you are.

No more silencing, no more dimming your light. You are now free to be who you came to be. Free to speak your heart and express your truth.

You are loved and always one with me. Let's go out and play. I want to see the world of wonders through your eyes.

We are a team now, unbreakable, and victorious.

I am a spiritual leader, teacher, mentor, psychic, and multi-dimensional healer. I'm the voice of the divine feminine and embodiment of divine grace, here to lead you back into wholeness to enable you to live your highest soul potential and wildest dreams.

It's my greatest passion to assist you in discovering your unique gifts and talents and guide you home to your natural state of divine joy. To assist you in removing everything, that prevents you from living your fullest potential, so you can step into divine leadership in service to God.

I have 14 years of experience empowering my soul tribe to greater joy, passion, and soul fulfillment on all levels of their life, to greater health and wealth. My gift is to tap into and pinpoint where you are sabotaging and withholding love to yourself. I've assisted thousands in healing from deep trauma, including sexual abuse, addictions, and self-destructive behaviors to catalyze radical and rapid quantum shifts in their lives. I help identify where you're giving your power away and refrain from making healthy choices and why.

I work on multiple levels to clear wounds from this and previous lifetimes and to facilitate groundbreaking results by clearing old vows, agreements, and mindsets holding you back from stepping into your full potential. I'm here to guide you through the dark night of the soul to reclaim your true might and light.

I'm available for one-on-one sessions, and mentorship programs and facilitate group activations and retreats.

Connect with Grace:

For bookings and more information go to my website:

www.graceelohim.com or write to info@graceelohim.com

Follow me on Facebook:

https://www.facebook.com/grace66solaris/

Visit my Soundcloud for free guided meditations:

https://soundcloud.com/grace-solaris

Listen to some interviews to get to know me better on my YouTube channel:

https://www.youtube.com/@graceelohim1/featured

"Oh yes said love. You can try to run away from me, but I will wait in your sacred heart like a patient lover until you return to me. I will never give up on you, I am who you truly are."

~ Grace Solaris

CHAPTER 12

RECAPITULATION BIRTHS ZERO POINT STILLNESS

HOW TO GET HERE, STAY HERE, AND MODEL IT

Jennifer Falchi

My Story

"You've got three minutes to make a list of your life's defining moments."

I flipped to a clean page in my notebook.

"Go."

Resistance swirled inside me.

I don't want to do this.

Going back there feels pointless.

I twirled my pen to release escalating agitation.

I need a story for this chapter.

"Okay. Wrap up your last thought."

My paper was as blank as my mind.

I had nothing.

Nothing?

Oh, wait a second.

There were no defining moments.

Could this be the end?

No more digging, recycling, or regurgitating the past.

Yes! I feel complete with it all.

I give myself permission to be done.

Done.

This was the conscious critical point where it wasn't possible to return to the previous state of being.

Giving myself full permission to unwaveringly declare 'the end' meant I understood that it was over on all levels. I could reset myself to version 2.0 and start this new chapter in my life—one of internal freedom and authentic ability to choose my next experience.

Writing my last chapter conveyed how I exited the world of mistreatment and no longer allowed myself to be subjugated. Submitting it for publishing officially shut the door, locked it, and threw away the key to the inner archive of stories centered around lack, control, and suffering; the painful trifecta of the human experience. These stories, their themes unfolding in endless dramas, were the hub of my existence. The details anchored, guided me, and informed my next steps. Movement translated into progress. It didn't matter I was wading knee-deep in the cesspools of Dante's Circles of Hell.

The barrage of suffering told me I was alive.
This was the ultimate addiction.

Somewhere, I signed up for a cosmic treatment plan to release this dependency.

Recent experiences in Teotihuacán codified the process I stumbled through for years, providing me with language, context, and a conscious experience of how this release works. The Toltecs, Mayans, and Aztecs called the cure for suffering, recapitulation.

I stepped out of my past by revisiting each experience without intertwining with, attaching to, or yearning for it. Reviewing an event like this opened the door to releasing the trapped emotional energy (memory holds emotions and self-limiting beliefs), which unhooked me from it. My light bytes were reclaimed and everything else returned to the source as all drama ended, traumas were cleared, and the fear that filled every single cell of me in all waking and sleeping moments vanquished. My inner world became quiet with nothing to feed the wheel of movement; no crisis to manage, nothing to chase, fix, or solve. Like a washing machine stuck on the spin cycle, once unplugged it stopped.

Hitting the reset button returned me to the beginning of it all, the void.

An energy center that's the source of all that is—zero point stillness, conscious ground zero—where nothing is everything and I have access to pure potential to create anything I desire.

The present moment where peace surpasses all understanding—the space between fear of the past and the anxiety of the future.

A stillness that allows the all-knowing heart to speak and guide, instead of habituated patterns of the mind and emotions, ensuring I flow toward life in each new moment with intentionality and sovereignty.

I occasionally visited this space in meditation.

How do I stay here without going back to bang on the door?

Holy Presence

These are my acts of power that anchor me into zero-point stillness:

- Maintain an inner stillness that invites a presence to ensure I move with my inner authority, my tether.

- Commit to preserving my status as a limitless being.
- Observe and listen to me carefully, with interest and attention, focusing particularly on the internal fluctuations of my mind.
- Circumvent any unconscious motivators and manage my life's energy, direction, and movement.

I feel safe enough now to shift the 24/7 hypervigilance to a focus on my inner landscape. My awareness is sharper with the new contrast between habituated movement and conscious choice, where the silence of truth rests in between.

The process of stripping down to nothing, diffusing one event at a time, gifted me with a plethora of knowledge on my inner workings. An advantage over my ego mind as I use the space inside to explore how sophisticated and sneaky my mind loops are and what unexpected things trigger them.

Look how fear controls me.
This fuels my reactions.
Here's why I've got the compulsion to do, do, do, and operate from my brain.
I see what motivates me to mind other people's business.
Mistrusting my inner authority starts here.

I choose to manage my mind because the mind games I play with myself are real and consequential.

The ego, the restrictive part of my mind, continues to misinform me that I'm in the wrong place, doing the wrong thing at the wrong time, and triggers memories that hold limiting beliefs and spike sensations. Awakening the four-letter F word (F-E-A-R) catapults me out of zero-point stillness to seek false security and control in a linear, rigid structure.

I have episodes of zero-point-less-ness. Speeding down cosmic Interstate 144 of life, enjoying the scenery, I'm as carefree as can be. It takes one moment to downshift into a distraction that renders my GPS (Genuine Present Self) offline and causes me to jerk the steering wheel to the closest exit. Here's my latest departure.

Soul speaks: *Don't buy it! Put the chips back on the shelf.*

My writing wasn't flowing. Agitation inspired a trip to the store.

Ego mind: *Let's get these cookies too.*

It was all in slow motion. The loop was familiar. I felt each step bring me further down a road with a lot of mileage.

I stopped the cart and considered doing this differently.

Soul speaks: *Leave the chips and the cookies here.*

Ego mind: *Just put one of them back.*

I put the chips back on the shelf.

Soul speaks: *Good choice! The salt dehydrates your eyes.*

I added fresh kale to cover the cookies.

Soul speaks: *Put the cookies back too.*

Ego mind: *No, I'll eat two for the next 12 days.*

I slinked to the checkout, knowing the truth.

I felt uncomfortable as I slowly slid them to the cashier, using the big bags of celery and carrots as decoys.

By evening, there was a fortnight's bag worth of emptiness.

I woke up the next morning terrorized by nightmares and old beliefs telling lies that I'm incapable, powerless, and unable to find my way out. Fear exacerbated subtle body tension constricting my ability to move my eyes, neck, and shoulders.

I devoted the morning to clearing my amnesia so I could remember who I am. I set up a sacred space and sat quietly to tune into what I needed. It took 30 minutes to override all the distractions and allow my physical body to find relief in the stillness.

Ping. Ping. Ping.

The disabled pop-up blockers that prevented my mind's advertisements were goading me to step out of stillness.

It's boring.
I don't want to do this.
Let's go back to bed. Then you'll feel fine.

There were shiny, sparkly visual cues calling me, feigning purposeful movement.

Look, the sun is shining! Let's play.
My glass is half empty.
The water table sheets are crooked.

The habit of checking the quiet cell phone every ten seconds was resolved by shutting it off.

Another 30 minutes passed as I continued working with Resonance Alchemy syllables.

This isn't working.

My ego mind intervened again, fed up with the same old imbalances my pendulum testing showed.

Addiction points again?
You must be doing something wrong.
Someone else needs to work on you.
When was the last time you had a healing session?
There's the problem.
I started to look at my calendar and brainstorm who could help me.

My inner witness observed this and I started laughing.

Nice try.
I am a healer.
What I facilitate for others, I can do for myself.

Now that I was more aware, it was easy to commit to more time. It became fun.

I learned a lot. Not quitting but committing, opened up healing. The core issue had nothing to do with writing. The last chapter I re-submitted stirred within me deep remembrances of feeling unsafe and shameful.

At the two-hour mark, tension began to release within my neck, shoulders, and third eye. Anchoring in the outer and inner stillness and becoming fully present created the synergy needed to create a state of balance.

In another 30 minutes, I felt clear and alert. I was ready to close this activity. Presence got me presents. Not the things I wanted to hop up and have at the start, but more valuable attributes of peace and calm.

Since I skipped my daily dose of frequency medicine for six days the rebalance required more effort. There were many early warnings.

Immediately noticing the initial rising sensations or emotions would've slammed on the brakes at the end of the exit ramp and brought me immediately back onto the highway. I blew past this sign. Identifying emotional cues eluded me most of my life or I mistakenly believed they meant something. They don't.

Disbelieving the ego mind's messages as truth, insisting I hurry up because time was running out would've meant exiting for a short rest stop and returning without delay. Time's the keyword since it's a limitation while flow is open, endless, and expansive.

I could've stayed on the highway by simply changing the lanes in my mind and telling my ego to shut up.
I have the ultimate authority to manage my mind, not my ego.

Instead, it took physical limitations, my body screaming for my attention and several days off the highway, lost on backroads. The crunch of the cookies was loud yet not enough to remind me that actively seeking comfort outside of myself was a clear sign I was out of zero-point stillness.

Did I mess up?

Nope.

I made a choice, had an experience, and then chose another one.

I am a powerful creator.
This is the gift in each moment.
Choice.

This experience was comprised of many choices, woven together to create a learning opportunity. It was clear how I got lost and what it took to get back on the interstate (much faster than the last time), and it reinforced the need to take action at the first warning sign. My mile markers are: Remember—Recognize—Release or Reroute—Reset—Roll.

The Medicine

The ego mind's stealth and the rapid movement from one moment to the next create a vulnerability for imbalance; however, rebalance is quickly possible. There are tools and practices to ensure you find zero-point stillness, stay here, and model it for others. I will share these in the next three sections.

LOSE YOUR MIND

Mundane activities like cooking, vacuuming, and cleaning, with a shift in perception, can perpetuate a mindless state and with imagination can be fun! Being outdoors and focusing on an aspect of beauty like birds singing or the way sunlight glistens like diamonds on rippling blue water resets your natural state. Finding an activity or learning something new, like croquet, strengthens focus, and concentration, and assigns the mind a new task.

When I've completely lost my mind, I hear the hum of my juicer, my mind translates life's details into a comedy, inciting laughter and I notice eagles flying over my head.

What are your indicators?

STRENGTHEN YOUR FOUNDATION

These tools are essential and as integral in each moment as my heartbeat. I can't 'be' without them.

A conscious intentional breath clears, creates space, and expands awareness. Find one you like or learn a new one. You can experiment with my 6-Pointed Lotus Breath practice, published in the book, Sacred Rebel, Chapter 12.

Things are always in a constant state of motion and trusting what you see, including yourself, is a challenge. I experience Spatial Referencing as a technique that provides a way to define your location in space and time and increases self-observation. Explore this through Xponential Intelligence podcasts Part 1, Episode #2.13 and Part 2, Episode #2.14 on YouTube.

TAKE YOUR FREQUENCY MEDICINE

The only valuable asset you have is your frequency, the strength that your light shines. You have a responsibility to raise it so you shine brighter and spark others!

Resonance Alchemy*, a frequency healing technique founded and developed by Katherine Parker, uses sacred healing syllables from a universal language of spirit. Through silent repetition (eight times minimum), the syllables create a resonant vibrational field, (similar to a tuning fork), to clear, vitalize, and retune your fields.

Most syllable phrases correspond to a point on or just off the body or stand alone as powerful Divine Essences. Sets of three to six-syllable phrases, called a Unified Healing Code (UHC), work together to focus on an aspect of healing. There are over 200! I love how they each tell a healing story.

Here's an experience with a protocol called Loving the Whole, the way I enjoy it. An opportunity to experience stillness while strengthening the partnership with your holy presence or inner witness as you practice 'inner listening' and notice what comes to light in your consciousness that isn't from a place of wholeness and love. You'll use this information and activate the healer within to elevate your frequency.

The protocol steps are: prepare your mind and body, open the Template of Healing points and those applicable to this UHC, repeat the syllables, and complete the process.

To access a recording and diagram of the Template of Healing points, click here: jennfalchi.com

LOVING THE WHOLE

Materials

A quiet sacred space, notebook, pen, and glass of water.

Preparation

1. Record what you are currently experiencing, without thinking.

   - Relax and take a few conscious breaths.
   - What do you notice?
   - Focus on emotional states, thoughts, feelings, or sensations that are arising.
   - Where are they in your body?
   - Name any sensations or emotions.

2. Create your intention and record it.

OPEN THE TEMPLATE OF HEALING POINTS

These are nine points on the body that when activated help to access all levels of your energy field.

There are two steps to activating these points, notifying your energy fields that you want to work with them. It's similar to clicking on a computer file.

It opens and then you can access the contents.

1. Tap the point(s) nine times to open them.
2. {Enter}* to inform your conscious and unconscious levels you want to access.

{Enter}* means tapping two places simultaneously, nine times:

1. Master Self point (top of sternum/below collarbone midline) with your right hand
2. Master Healing point (three fingers below navel) with your left hand

TAP THE TEMPLATE OF HEALING POINTS:

1. Main Energy Channels (each one, nine times)

- Core Channel (Energy of Oneness), top of head
- Holographic Cosmic Template (Energy of Divine Mind), top of forehead at hairline
- Right and Left Channels (Masculine and Feminine Energy), midpoint above each eyebrow

{Enter}*

2. Master Center points (each one nine times)

- Master Spin (Super-conscious Mind), center of forehead
- Master Self (Conscious Mind), top of sternum/below collarbone midline
- Master Soul (Subconscious Mind), center of the diaphragm
- Master Healing (Unconscious Mind), three fingers below the navel

{Enter}*

3. Heart Field (nine times)

(Energy of Relating, Connects & Unifies All Parts of the Whole), above the left breast using your whole hand

{Enter}*

- ○ Rest
- ○ Take a few conscious breaths between each of the three sets.
- ○ Reflect on your experience.
- ○ What is happening inside of you?
- ○ Do you sense energy moving?
- ○ How do you feel?

PRACTICE LOVING THE WHOLE UNIFIED HEALING CODE

Below are four syllables phrases {Syllable/Meaning}, each with a truth statement.

(Pronunciation tips: A is 'aah' as in father; 'O' as in flow; 'U' as in glue; and 'OK' rhymes with clock)

- DWAL OK/Seeing With New Eyes

  Truth: I see you

- DU'MOR/Unification of Perception

  Truth: I understand you

- KRI LEI AMMA/Unconditional Love

  Truth: I love you unconditionally

- REYA CHO/Radiant Wholeness

  Truth: You are whole

1. Tap the corresponding point for this UHC.

- Master Self point, nine times

  {Enter}*

  ○ Do this two more cycles while focusing on your intention.

2. Start with the first syllable phrase and say it out loud. Say the corresponding meaning.

   (Example: DWAL OK/Seeing With New Eyes)
   ○ Rest quietly.

3. Next, use the pre-fix KRI AM A'LA'TUR and add the first syllable to it.

   (Example: KRI AM A'LA'TUR DWAL OK)

Say this quietly to yourself, eight times, for a total of 24-48 times.
   ○ Focus on the feelings, and places in your body with sensations.

   ○ Speak directly to the inner part of you.

○ Inhale and exhale slowly.

4. Say the truth statement.

5. Rest and observe.

6. Repeat steps 1-5 with the second, third, and fourth syllables.

7. Allow processing time.

8. Repeat steps 1-5, as many times as needed.

9. When you feel complete, repeat AMORE CHO RAE, once
   (Loving the Expression of the Whole)

10. End this UHC with AL TOR KRI AM TUR MAK (three times)
    ○ This supercharges the syllables.

{Enter}*

COMPLETION

Congratulations! You've taken your frequency medicine!

○ Write about your experience

○ Hydrate and nurture yourself

○ Look in the mirror and admire your sublime radiance

MORE UNIFIED HEALING CODES!

Practice these as inspired.

Follow steps #1 to #10 above, omitting #4 and #9.

Forgiveness

Tap below left collarbone

DUR AM ZAR/Lightness of Being, Freedom from the Past

AB BA/Joy, Light Heart

KAR LA'AM HOUR/Balance of Giving and Receiving, Justice

ARTH RECHT/Righteousness, Alignment with Universal Law

Emotional Pain Clearing

Tap Heart field

ALARA RAM/Mercy, Divine Blessing

SA LA'AM/Wellbeing

LEI MAR BA LOR TA'AM/Interdependence

Mental Pattern Clearing

Tap any Master Point

A KEEM DU GUAL/Mediation, Active Intelligence of Balanced Perspective

ZA' KEEM/Learning, Acquired Knowledge, Skill

DU' TUR RAM/Transformation, Transformative Process

DWAL MOG/Radiant Emptiness

DWAK OK/Seeing with New Eyes

*Parker, Katherine. Resonance Alchemy: *Awakening The Tree of Life*. Balboa Press, 2013.

Jenn Falchi is a gifted luminary, catalyst, and alchemist whose activations and experiences span four continents. Her commitment to decades of self-discovery illuminating, excavating, and healing her own shadow creates a bridge for authentic rapport. With deep wisdom gained in roles as mother, daughter, sister, Peace Corps volunteer, executive, and spiritual warrior, she is known as an empoweress who shares keys and codes to unlock innate healing capabilities, expand consciousness, ignite unlimited potential, and elucidate longings deep within one's soul. She's a beacon of strength, honesty, and encouragement.

Jenn's a trusted companion who guides curious, sincere seekers on a journey through their unexplored inner landscape. It begins with a sacred conversation. With clients as co-authors, she facilitates organic experiences unique to each person's desired exploration of a body, mind, or spirit aspect. She and the journeyers map the expedition, recalibrate GPS to true north, and inspect baggage to lighten the load. Together they clear energetic highways, tune-up vehicle bodies for efficiency, and create unlimited supplies of quantum fuel. Everyone receives personalized healing tools to support smoother navigation in life.

Through the perfect combination of frequency medicine, somatic practices, and subconscious work, a client achieves an optimal balance of their nervous system, clears stress, anxiety, and trauma, and anchors more peace, harmony, and balance as blocked energy is shifted with sound and light. Experiences are offered in person or remotely and tailored for couples, groups, and businesses.

Jenn earned certifications to facilitate:

Resonance Alchemy (https://resonancealchemy.com)

Quantum Energy Coaching (https://qecliving.com)

LaHo-Chi Energy (https://lahochi.org)

When Jenn isn't swimming in the Albemarle Sound with mermaids, whacking croquet balls across Doodle Hill, or cracking herself up with the divine comedy of life, she'd love to connect with you here:

Connect with Jenn:

Website: www.jennfalchi.com

Facebook: www.facebook.com/jennfalchi

LinkedIn: https://www.linkedin.com/in/jennifer-falchi-4b606415

Email: sublimeradiance144@gmail.com

I am a powerful creator.
This is the gift in each moment.
Choice.

~ Jenn Falchi

CHAPTER 13

FROM FLIGHT TO FIGHT

TRANSMUTING TRAUMA INTO STRENGTH

Kristina Dubois, BSc. C.H.N.C.

My Story

**"Say it!" he screamed.
"Say it and I'll let you get up. Tell me that you do not believe in God!"**

I could feel the weight of his hands pressing down onto my shoulders as he straddled my small frame.

"No," I whispered. "I can't say that."

The pressure in my head increased from trying to hold back the tears that threatened to come. I could feel his impatience growing stronger. The vein bulged above his left temple as his face became more crimson with each breath. We had been at this standstill now for what felt like an eternity. At first, I tried to struggle against him. The competitive weightlifter was winning. My struggle was futile.

He took a deep breath and tried to regain some composure. His face softened as his grip on my arms lessened. "Why do you believe in God?" he asked. "How can you believe in God? Give me proof, evidence."

"How can you not?" I replied. In my 21-year-old mind, I didn't believe anyone could truly be an atheist. Surely not the man I'd chosen to commit myself to.

"There's no scientific evidence," he said. "If you can give me scientific evidence, then you can believe in God." I feel my body go limp. I close my eyes. My heart is pounding in my ears as I retreat into my own thoughts. My thoughts are scattered, going in a million different directions.

How can someone else tell me what to think?
That's not okay. Why do I have to justify my beliefs?
Please let the baby wake up. Then surely, he will let me go get the baby.
How can I make this stop?

"Sometimes you don't need scientific evidence to believe something," I finally whisper as my heart sinks.

He disagrees. I feel my eyes burning and I can't hold back the tears anymore. My tears escape from the corners of my eyes and start to slide down the sides of my face. Silence permeates the room, as he steadily maintains his position of power over me, on all levels–physically, emotionally, and even spiritually.

I look away in submission. I can't meet his gaze anymore. A cry breaks the silence. The baby is awake. I look expectantly back at my husband. "Just say it," he says one more time. "Tell me you don't believe in God, then we can get the baby."

I look away. It's at this moment that I choose to give my power away.

"Fine," I say dejectedly. "I don't believe in God," I whisper in a voice low enough, that just maybe God will not hear.

I was never the athletic girl.
The sporty girl.
I was the smart girl.
The academic.

As a child I'd always choose quiet activities. I found solace in my books. That was my quiet time, a time to recharge. I was usually smaller than most girls my age and never thought of myself as being physically strong. As the daughter of a Marine, I didn't need to be strong. Boys were supposed to be strong. Girls were supposed to be smart. That's the story I created for over 40 years. It seemed to be true in my childhood home, and that narrative continued when I married a competitive weightlifter.

Years later, that marriage fell apart, and I was left on my own, as a single mother of four. I went back to school and got a Bachelor of Health Science. *Surely that'll solve all my problems—get smarter.* Surprisingly, it didn't.

I watched as my parents' health deteriorated and my father, the strongest man I ever knew, fall and eventually die from complications of a hip fracture.

After his fall, I had to take a good hard look at myself. *What happened to me over the years?* Despite everything I did, I struggled to achieve balance. *Do I want to end up like my parents?* I gained a significant amount of weight and didn't even recognize myself anymore. In the spring of 2019, I joined a gym. I joined gyms in the past, and paid membership fees for years, but seldom, if ever, went.

I vowed to myself; *this time would be different.*

At first, this was a journey of health. I committed to going three times a week. I did for the first while, but then life got in the way, as it always does. I started nutrition school and dropped to twice a week. COVID arrived and gave me an excellent excuse to abandon my commitment to my body for a year and a half, even though I saw the results of more energy and changes in my body form.

In the spring of 2021, COVID restrictions were lifted, and I went back to the gym. This time I committed to five days a week. When I went before, my three-day commitment was easy to let slide. "Oh, I'm tired, I'll just go tomorrow," or "I want to meet a friend," or any other excuse as a reason to turn around. *There's always tomorrow.*

The transformation started happening when I decided to go every day. It became a routine; it was just what I did after work. I didn't have to think about it; I just went. I started looking forward to going to the gym,

I consistently felt better after each workout, and I enjoyed the extra energy I never had before.

My mindset shifted again, and I realized that hour in the gym could be mine.

It became self-care. In my busy life, it's the one moment a day I have completely to myself. My thoughts are my own, and I'm able to leave work and home behind. It became a meditative practice, and the most important part of my day.

Slowly, my body started to change once again. I developed strength I didn't know I could. At almost 50 years old, I'm as strong as any of the younger girls in that gym. I can see muscle definition for the first time in my life. The physical strength I've gained helped me to gain balance. I'm now stronger, not only physically but mentally and emotionally. But I still can't do a cartwheel!

Physical strength has given me the ability to reclaim and efficiently manage the parts of myself I lost.

The Medicine

Unless you've been living under a rock, you've probably heard of the fight or flight response. This is the body's response to a threat, either perceived or real. It's a stress response. It's an important mechanism when stress is short-lived, but becomes problematic during times of chronic stress. When this response is triggered, your hormone balance is thrown off, and your adrenal glands start to overproduce cortisol and adrenaline. Short-term, this is great.

For our ancestors, it helped them get away from that tiger chasing them or to fight off invading predators. Unfortunately, our bodies don't recognize the difference between stress caused by these types of isolated incidents and the modern stresses we encounter every day. Trauma leads to stress. Often, the stress induced by trauma doesn't just go away when the incident is over. Just as we hold onto the trauma, our body continues to function as if under stress. The results of this on the body over time lead to dysfunction, dysregulation, and disease. Just look around. Our modern population is plagued by an epidemic of obesity, diabetes, anxiety, depression, heart disease, hypertension, and even cancers. What do all these things have in common? They can all be linked to high levels of cortisol. Why does the stress caused by trauma lead to sustained levels of cortisol in the long term? Because trauma changes how we think. It changes how we perceive the world. It teaches us to live in a world of fear where we don't ever feel completely safe. We learn not to let our guard down. And the body responds accordingly.

If we hope to change this response, we need to first deal with the trauma. Trauma is never two-dimensional. It's always multi-faceted and as such you need to take a multi-faceted approach to deal with past trauma. Unless you address the trifecta of mind, body, and spirit, you'll never resolve the trauma.

**In order to make a change,
you must first decide that you're going to make a change.
While it's not easy, it can be done.**

The first step is to be honest with yourself.

Then, ask yourself the following questions:

- What is it that needs to change?
- Why do you need to make a change?
- What would it look like if you made the change?
- Who will this change affect in your world?
- When will you start to implement these changes? Are you ready to take action and take back your power?

I would argue that "why" is the most important question of all. Without this answer, the rest is moot.

Only when you can self-reflect and answer these questions honestly, will you even be able to consider change.

Are you ready to step into your authenticity and accept yourself as you truly are?

This is the space where transformation can begin.

The thing about addressing trauma is that there are just as many ways to address the trauma as there are people in this world. The answer is going to be unique to each individual. The way that you decide to approach this is going to be different than the way that I have decided to approach it. We all experience trauma at some point in our lives.

None of us leave this planet unscathed.

I encourage you to try many different things to find the thing or the combination of things that'll work for you. There's counseling, and counseling absolutely helps, but even with counseling, unless you're ready to do the work, it will have limited effectiveness. I'm a strong advocate for counseling, and I do believe that for many it can and should be part of your approach to healing trauma. Just know that it's not a magic pill.

There are no magic pills.
The medicine is in the work you choose to do.
Its effectiveness will match the energy that you put in.
If you want extra-strength medicine, be willing to put in extra energy!

Let's talk meditation. What does meditation mean to you? Consider what comes to mind for you when you hear the word *meditation*. A lot of people will picture an individual sitting in the traditional lotus position, perfectly still, legs crossed, hands on the knees, possibly even chanting the familiar, "OM," in the perfect tone. Yes, this is a form of meditation for some, and yes, this is practiced worldwide. Traditional meditation, breathwork, and yoga, are all taught as forms of meditation to still the mind and calm the nervous system.

Do these work? Absolutely.
Do they work for everyone? Absolutely not.

If those methods haven't worked for you, I'm going to ask you to consider another definition of meditation. Maybe it doesn't have to be sitting in a lotus position. Maybe it isn't about chanting "OM," or other mantras. Maybe it isn't attending meditation classes or using a meditation app. Maybe it isn't about trying to force a stillness that doesn't want to come. Maybe it's a little more organic than that.

Let's consider meditation in broader terms.

Think about a child, for example. A child who is outside riding a bike, playing in a sandbox, or spending time alone coloring. They don't seem to have a care in the world, but they are in their own little world. During this time, their brain has time to process. It may be processing the events of the day, the week, or an event they've experienced. This may all be happening unconsciously.

**For the child, this can be a form of meditation.
This happens for adults too.**

Ask yourself, *What do I like to do?* If you've forgotten what you enjoyed before life got in the way, try to remember what you liked to do once upon a time. Schedule time to try that activity. Be open to the fact that you might have to try a few things.

- Coloring - I suspect one of the reasons that adult coloring has gained such popularity in recent years is its ability to transport people to places of tranquility and meditation.

- Painting – This activity has been practiced for hundreds, if not thousands of years as an expression of the subconscious mind.

- Baking – This simple act requires attention and focus, while contributing to a family or greater community. Many people find this to be therapeutic.

- Journaling – Journaling can offer a great release of emotion and experiences, if you allow yourself to relax into the writing and be vulnerable.

- Running – Running offers a great release for many, which not only strengthens you mentally, but physically as well.

- Biking – This is another physical activity many people can use to calm their nervous system.

- There are countless activities that you can try, and come up with your own combination of what is effective for you.

Maybe you don't like the things you once did, and it's time to try something new. That's okay. Accept yourself for who you truly are today and be open to change. You need to find a space where meditation can happen naturally.

**Be conscious about the unconscious.
Find an activity where you can go into a meditative space.
It will be transformative for you.**

I found that in the gym. In the gym, I've been able to address the mind and body components of my being. It has helped me to rise above my trauma. This has not happened overnight. It has taken four years. The first two were about learning to change my mindset and subsequently choosing to make a commitment. This commitment was to myself and to my health and became a journey of wellness. Initially, I went three times a week, but that wasn't a commitment. That was me saying, *I'll do it when I have time, when there's nothing better to do.*

The truth is, there's always something better to do, so this left lots of room for excuses. *I'm tired today. I didn't sleep well last night. I have had a long day. I can just go tomorrow.*

**I had to change my mindset.
If this was going to work, I had to make this a lifestyle.**

I made a conscious decision to go five days a week. It wasn't until I committed that I was able to make a change. It wasn't until I committed that I learned the power of mindfulness. Every day after work, I got in my car and drove in the opposite direction of my home. I drove to the gym. There was no more mental discussion of if I would go, or have an excuse to put it off. I chose to make this part of my routine. I chose to make this part of what I do and who I am. That conscious decision is when my transformation began. I have a supportive environment where the owner cares about her clients. She has often held workshops for her members on mindfulness, meditation, and motivation.

When I enter the gym, in my mind I create a space just for me. In this space, I can forget the stresses of everyday life. I leave my home life, work life, family, and friends at the door.

That hour is my time and space, where nothing else exists.

I go into a meditative space. When I do this successfully, I can push my body and my mind to reach new levels. I challenge myself mentally to push through things I once only dreamed of being able to do on a physical level. I can process events of the day and past events on a subconscious level. This space even allows me to explore deeper levels of faith, and what it means to me. In my gym time, I find the intersection of body, mind, and spirit, where I am whole. I can transcend the limiting beliefs I once held, and in doing so, I begin to reverse the effect of past traumas. Sometimes this process is conscious, and sometimes it's subconscious, but both are necessary.

This has been my journey to wellness.

Kristina Dubois, BSc. C.H.N.C., was born in the Gatineau Hills of Quebec, Canada, spending her formative years moving between Ontario, Quebec, and New York State, before settling in Calgary, Alberta, with her family at the age of 12. She attended Mount Royal University where she obtained her Bachelor of Science with a major in Health Science. She then furthered her studies through the Canadian School of Natural Nutrition, becoming certified as a Holistic Nutritional Consultant. She is currently employed by a national non-profit organization where she has worn many different hats, including working with children, being a community liaison between marginalized populations and other community support groups, and most recently acting as a Community Program Coordinator.

In addition to this, Kristina has studied the Usui System of Natural Healing, to gain the distinction of Reiki Master. She also worked extensively with Angel Rohrer and has the honor of being one of the first Priestess initiates of the Nina Songo Energy Medicine Mystery School. She is a lifelong learner and believes that exploring the mind-body-spirit connection is the key to living a long and prosperous life.

Kristina currently lives in Calgary with her youngest son and cat and keeps herself busy by going to the gym and spending time with friends. She also loves to recharge with a cup of tea, a furry blanket, and a good book.

Connect with Kristina at:

Website: kosmicvitality.com

Email: admin@kosmicvitality.com

"Be conscious about the unconscious."

~ Kristina Dubois

CHAPTER 14

WHY AVATARS SING

RESILIENCY BUILDING FOR THE UP-AND-COMING LEADER

Grace Kohn

My Story

Holding her legs in obvious visible pain, withering on the ground, I wondered for a moment: *Is she having a heart attack? Should I be calling 911 right now? No,* I kept hearing. *She is processing her grief. It's okay; everything is going to be okay. Trust your leadership.*

My friend asked me for a singing lesson—no—begged me for a singing lesson. She was all about it. "I want to take singing lessons from you; it's something I've wanted to do for a long time now; it's for me; I need to do it," she voiced.

"Okay, let's do it then," I replied.

And here we were not too far into it, and I was worried something had gone incredibly wrong. Thanks to that part of us (the Leader within) that seems to know what to do in times of crisis, I remained calm and encouraged her to take slow, deep, deliberate breaths.

She listened to my voice commands, "Breathe in, breathe out, breathe in, breathe out."

Slowly, she regained her composure, but her hands were still clutching her heart.

We aren't out of the woods yet, I thought.

Intuitively, I knew what was coming up for her was deep grief in her body, and even as I write this, confirmation in the form of tears rising in my eyes occurs. She's my reflection and probably yours if you're reading this.

None of us are out of the woods yet, are we? It's been an intense couple of years for everyone.

If anything, these past couple of years has thrown us around like a Raggedy Ann doll. Our nervous systems have been in a fight, flight, and more fear zone continuously. Who to believe and what to listen to has challenged us all. If you haven't lost one relationship over the past few years, consider yourself lucky.

"So how is singing going to help me?" you ask. "Trust my leadership," is my simple request.

It's been found that the ancients sang. They sang even before they spoke, apparently. They sang in groups and together in caves, often. The resonance they developed between themselves cemented their connection to each other and the group. Like a forest, when roots connect, information can travel quickly to all members. I bring up the woods because, as we all know, yet often forget, it's because of our tree family we can even function on this Earth. Every time we breathe in, it's because an exchange with a tree's out-breath occurred. Whether we think about it or not, we depend on trees to keep us alive. We can do without food, even water for long periods, but a few minutes without air, baby, and you're somewhere else. Breathwork is as essential to singing as mycelium is to healthy forests. It's about connections. To become a successful leader, you must connect to your body. You hold the medicine.

Your body is intelligent. We often think all our intelligence comes from our brains. Yes, there is, of course, that type of intelligence. There is heart intelligence as well. Many organizations like HeartMath have and are proving the intelligence of the heart. Thirdly, your body has intelligence. From my observations, this last area has received the least attention. With today's use of technology, more and more people seem to be less and less in their bodies and more in their heads. With their screens in their hands, often from morning to night, we lose our connection to our body intelligence. Singing reconnects you to that intelligence because your body is the instrument. It would be best if you were as grounded, rooted as a giant oak, to sing. In fact, the more grounded you are, the more extensive your vocal range will be, the more strength your voice will have, and the more flexibility you'll have to play with sound. As we strengthen these areas, we affect how we live our lives, who we become, and how we lead.

Back to my friend, after we rebalanced her breathing, I invited her to tone some sounds. The first sound I asked her to join me in was AH. AH, pronounced AWE, is connected to our hearts. Every time we make the sound AH, our hearts are positively affected.

After AH, we played with OH and then Ooo. I recently discovered that Noo is an ancient word meaning primordial waters. *(*Secret Doctrine*, H.P. Blavatsky).

Ooo, pronounced as you would, the word "new" had a dramatic effect on my friend, particularly on her inner waters. Like a backed-up sink, the block in her heart area needed to be unplugged, and the miracle was that it was her very own singing voice that did just that.

The Ancients mapped out all the lines and energy centers in our bodies. Some cultures call the energy that runs through these lines and centers *chi,* and others call it *prana*. Regardless of what you call it, the bottom line is that when we get blocked in any of these areas, we have dis-ease and definite discomfort. These blocks, as I was recently reminded by my Pleiadian friend Barbara Marciniak *(*"Bringers of the Dawn"*) are primarily emotional in nature. If we're not allowed to express our emotions freely, they get backed up into the pipes. Eventually, if too much gets stuffed down there, kaboom! You have a big mess.

The ancients knew sounding could help clear unexpressed anger, rage, sadness, guilt, and grief and even alleviate depression. The beauty is we have the ability right inside to help ourselves. I'm happy to report my friend lived that day; I didn't call an ambulance. She walked out the door on her own accord, humming the tune of a song we worked on later that session.

Because our singing voice is so deeply connected to our soul, singing can activate powerful initiations in your body.

Just recently, another friend of my mine was over for her lesson. As we made our way through various songs, we reached a point in the class where the sun was strongly streaming through a nearby window. The sun hit me first, and I immediately wanted my friend to feel it, so I led her to stand in the sun with her drum. We continued to sing. We sang a very simple song. You may even know it. It's called: *It only takes a spark to get a fire going.*

My friend is very connected to fire and leads our weekly fire gatherings. Her reason for coming for singing lessons was so she'd feel comfortable leading the women in song at the fires. It's a pleasure to teach her, as she is so open to working past her comfort zone even if her monkey mind says she shouldn't.

As she was singing, she had an experience I'd call an initiation. It was about reconnecting parts of herself that had been split, possibly for a long time. As the words were spilling out of her mouth, she saw something in her mind's eye that penetrated her whole body deeply. She shared with me what she saw. Twenty-seven years ago, I had the same experience she was having; the only difference was I was alone and six months pregnant.

I write in-depth about this experience in my first bestselling book, *Children of Autumn – Autism Here on Purpose.* Because I had this background, I could assist her in integrating what was going on, which has profound implications for her moving forward.

The "I" of who we are comprises different parts. There is a masculine part and a feminine part. Often, people are working primarily from one aspect. To fully become whole, we need the two parts to reunite and be in balance. The initiation my friend was having was internally reconnecting these two aspects for her. Singing was the mechanism by which this occurred. When working as our whole selves, we're far more resilient and comfortable leading.

The Medicine

Having a child with Autism as well as a typical child, I've learned resiliency.

There are four primary components to becoming resilient.

1. The importance of connection.

2. Wellness.

3. Healthy thinking.

4. The meaning one has with life itself.

Let's explore number one and how it relates directly to singing. To be resilient, you need to have a solid connection to yourself, others, your community, your country, Spirit, and nature. Let's go back to our beautiful tree, friends. When you're singing, I strongly recommend you think of yourself as a tree and root yourself deep into the ground. Feel that you have roots coming out the bottom of your feet, connecting with all the other trees around you. Imagine you're relating to the trees you love the most. They're all beautiful, so pick your favorite. Take some time here to feel the co-creation between you and the type of tree you've chosen. Imagine it's in front of you, and as you breathe out, you can feel it breathe in. Likewise, as it breathes out, you feel it, and you breathe in. Trees can bend to great angles. They can withstand powerful gusts of wind. Becoming connected to the Earth in the form of a tree as a place to sing from will make you more resilient in all your endeavors.

How connected to others do you feel right now? On a scale of one to ten, ten being strongly connected, where would you rate yourself? Do not go into judgment based on what you give yourself. To be resilient, you need to feel connected to others. Singing can bring this about in many ways. You can quickly join a choir, band, drumming circle, a theatre group that puts on musicals, sing with the radio, sing with your children if you have children, or join our Singing Wolves group on Monday nights. Check out www.childrenofautumn.com for more information regarding this offering.

We need to feel a connection with community, so if you cannot find something directly in your physical community, join us online. The more we build these connections, the better for us all. Everybody needs a place to howl. You are most welcome.

Did you know trees sing? Seriously. I first heard them singing in a magical place called Damanhur in northern Italy. After working with plants for over 30 years, they developed a machine that you connect to a keyboard and then the plant directly. The electromagnetic field of the plant 'plays' the keyboard, or as I like to think of it, sings through the keyboard.

It's pretty amazing to witness. Once you've heard even one plant sing, it doesn't take much to imagine what an entire forest would sound like together.

Connecting to nature also improves your resiliency. If plants themselves sing, doesn't it make even more sense to immerse yourself outside by a campfire, a body of water, or deep in a forest and sing together with the elements? Fire is such a powerful element to sing with because you have that strong sun presence with you as well. Sun gives life to all natural things and will do the same for you. As the flames dance in front of you, and while different colors paint themselves around the coals for you, sing out to the stars, moon, and all the planets. We are part of a mysterious magnificent universe; we're here on purpose, and connecting to all these elements through song is one of the oldest and wisest ways of filling up one's battery pack.

WELLNESS AND RESILIENCY

You know you have a nervous system, but did you know it has different parts? One part is called the parasympathetic nervous system. It does its best to keep you in a relaxed state. If this system functions well, you'll feel emotionally, mentally, and physically healthier. When we're in a fight, flight, or fright mode, the sympathetic nervous system is active. Our parasympathetic nervous system kicks in and does something called down-regulating. Involved with the vagus nerve, which connects to your vocal cords and the muscles at the back of your throat, there are ways you can activate this nerve.

What can help you to down-regulate? Deep breathing, singing, and humming. It's scientifically proven that when people hum or sing, they positively affect their nervous system. Furthermore, according to Sarah Wilson, clinical neuropsychologist and head of the School of Psychological

Sciences at the University of Melbourne, "There is a singing network in the brain which is quite broadly distributed. When we speak, the hemisphere of the brain dealing with language lights up. When we sing, both sides of the brain spark into life. We also see the involvement of the feeling networks of the brain."

Lastly, singing is an aerobic exercise that creates the release of endorphins. Baishali Mukherjee, the Southeast Asia regional liaison for the World Federation of Music Therapy, shares, "The feeling of happiness we get from endorphins is associated with a reduction of stress. In any situation, whether it is under stress or with any physical ailments, illness, and/or psychological deprivation, music has the potential to affect our body immunity and mind positively."

HEALTHY THINKING AND RESILIENCY

Positive thinking, we know, affects our physiology by strengthening our immune system. To build your resiliency, sing songs of praise, inspiration, joy, gratitude, love, and communion.

LIFE MEANING

Viktor Frankl, an Auschwitz survivor, wrote a book called *Man's Search for Meaning.* He believed that humans are motivated by something he called a "Will to meaning." He argued that life could have meaning even in the most miserable circumstances and that the motivation for living comes from finding that meaning. My 93-year-old mother-in-law, who was locked in her small apartment for 21 days in complete isolation during the Canadian COVID lockdowns, found her meaning by teaching herself and singing many different hymns during those days. Her choosing this course of action kept her resilient and with us. Amazing!

This chapter aims to assist you as you evolve into the leadership role you're coded for by inspiring you to sing, hum, and practice deep breathing. Following are a few warmup ideas for you to play with.

The ancients knew the power of sound; they are whispering to you now: *It is your birthright to sing, be proud, and change the world with your voice!*

As you light up both sides of your brain, you light up the world! We need your voice. The time of the lone wolf is over. Reunite with your pack!

WARMUPS

- Breathe in through your nose and out through your mouth.

- Observe your breathing as it moves up and down your spine.

- Breathe deeply into your belly, and use the Yoga child's pose. The only place you can breathe from in this position is your belly.

- Relax, and warm up your lips, blowing them together as you did as a kid. Pretend to drive a motorcycle or truck around. Let your lips really vibrate together. Move your body around if you feel inspired to. Play with the sound coming from you going up and down like a scale while you blow your lips out.

- Give your jaw a nice gentle massage along the edges of it on both sides. Place your fingers on the edges and gently massage down to your chin. We hold a lot of stress in our jaws, so giving them a massage will feel great.

- You have three voices you can develop in your body: head, mid, and chest voice. Imagine you have a tube that is about two inches wide. It's very flexible and starts in the Earth. It comes through your body up the inside of you, like a channel, and out the top of your head. Every time you breathe in from the Earth, your breath rises through this tube, and when you make a sound, it's as if a key or a string has been played and is now resonating out through your mouth.

- Practice making the sound AH. When you make this sound, let your mouth drop open. Start using AH on any note you wish. Do this a few times, and if you can go up and down a few notes, that's great. If you have a musical instrument to use, please do. If you don't, there are numerous apps you can find to help you. VoCo, Sing Sharp, and SWIFTSCALES are a few.

- Next, experiment with Ooo. This sounds like "new." Play with the word *noo*. Give gratitude to a body of water you love, your favorite river, stream, creek, ocean, someone you love, or even yourself.

- Play with the sounds Eee, OH, I, and A similarly.

Unmask your avatar and sing! It's your birthright.

Singer, author, advocate, speaker, teacher, mother, and now farmer, **Grace** shares tools and strategies that have helped her to remain resilient, grounded, and loving in the face of challenges. As a parent of a beautiful adult daughter living with Autism, Grace has learned many valuable lessons through her adventures. Singing since she was a toddler, she today teaches both children and adults the power of singing and how it can transform us and connect us deeply to ourselves and others. Her daughter, Julianne, went from non-verbal at seven to a non-stop singer today.

Grace is the author of the bestselling book, *Children of Autumn - Autism Here on Purpose.* She offers a unique and hopeful message that reaffirms that Autism is here on purpose to help our species evolve and become more loving. Grace has delivered her message to various audiences, including teachers, healthcare professionals, parents, and other thought leaders. Many have found personal value and relevance to their own experiences even though they may not live with the challenge of Autism.

Grace is available for presentations to speak or sing anywhere in the world. She has presented in Canada and the United States. She lives with her Beloved in Jasper, Alberta, Canada, and recently opened the first Jule House—a unique home for special people. You can find her voice on Spotify as Griggs and Grace.

In 2022 she started the YouTube Channel "Grace, Marla, Nicole, and Friends," uniting children with nature through song, puppetry, and Drama. On this channel, children meet Elfie the Elephant and Koala, who together learn about nature, art, and our global family. If you have children or are just young at heart, you can find them @childrenofautumn.com on the YouTube. For more information and offerings, visit www.childrenofautumn.com.

"Be the Miracle"

~ Grace Kohn

CHAPTER 15

TRANSFORMATION THROUGH TOUCH

WHEN YOU ARE READY, YOUR TIMELINE WILL SHIFT

Emoke Molnar

My Story

**It was my turn to receive, I had everything under control.
I started to enjoy the pain, then everything shifted.
Here I am again on a different level.
I have lost control, and I am screaming my lungs out for help!**

You reach a certain point in your life when you know it is time to make a decision. I remember the day when I decided to follow my intuition and chose to learn something new. I signed up for a holistic massage course, knowing I needed to take action and show up.

I signed up without even thinking.
I did not take the time to see what I had signed up for.
I did not read the instructions on what to bring to class.
I just knew when to show up.
I was not prepared for what was to come.

I arrived at the class. Butterflies were dancing in my stomach. *What am I supposed to do? What's going to happen?* We were asked to share about ourselves and at that moment, I had no idea what to say.

Oh my God! Will they be able to understand me? Is my English good enough? Who are all these people? Why do we have to share? I don't want to share! What the hell have I signed up for?

I started to see my classmates with different eyes as they shared from their hearts. *Clearly, they knew what they were signing up for.* These souls gathered in this space were courageous, full of love and wished to be in service as did I.

I started to feel a shift in the air. My eyes locked with the man sitting across the circle from me. *I know you will be my first partner.* I smiled as we were paired. *I wonder how many more times that is going to happen this week?* I thought as he started to practice on me.

My childhood memories started to poke into my consciousness as he worked through the teachings.

What is that mark on your head?
Are you strong enough to wear the name they are calling you?
Your mind is endless.

I see the gypsy woman who told me I am marked.
I see my mother throwing my Tarot decks into the fire.

Who am I? Why am I thinking about all these things?
Am I a witch, as the gypsy woman said?

As the lesson continued, I didn't have time to integrate what I had just experienced. Now, the tables had turned, and I was the one giving the massage.

I started to relax and enjoy the process of learning and was utterly amazed at how complex our bodies are. I wanted to absorb the teachings from these masters, even though I did not understand what was going on.

My turn on the table again! Not sure how I feel about this!

There I was, back on the table, the first in the class to start crying.

> *I'm so embarrassed! I don't want to cry! I'm so emotional.*
> *I can't wait for this day to be over!*
> *Will my warrior survive this?*

My partner was massaging my knees and I was thrust back in time to my father's funeral.

> *Why am I back at my father's funeral?*
> *What am I doing here? There is death all around me!*

"Breathe, breathe," I heard the teacher step in and whisper in my ear. "Come back," she whispered as she called me back to the present. I was safe. I did not need to fear death here. The poor guy working on me had no idea what was happening.

With the second day over, I was happy and relaxed. I survived day two!

I would not be so lucky the next day. I did not survive day three.

I'm losing my legs! Who is putting hot stones on my legs? Why isn't anyone helping me?! I feel myself leaving my body and I witness my anguish from the corner of the ceiling.

What is happening?

There are five people around the massage table. Someone is dying on the table, and nobody is helping. *Does that person have no soul? Wait a minute, that's me! That's my body! I must go back to it. How do I get back to it?*

"Help me before I lose my legs!" I begged my teacher. "Something is on my legs!"

"There is nothing on your legs; just breathe, breathe, breathe," she says as I feel myself drop back into my body.

I open my eyes to witness my teachers surrounding me. *I'm so confused. I don't understand what is happening.*

I feel an energy with a purple light rushing through my body. Trying to kill me.
Is this the end of my life?

Screaming, crying, *God, stop it before I die!*

Finally, I get a minute to breathe and rest into full bliss as my body starts to surrender. I allow my muscles to sink into the bed as my heart and breath slow down into stillness. Suddenly my senses become heightened as paralysis takes over my body.

Wait!
What's happening?
Oh no, here it comes again!

My breath quickens as the purple wave hits me again, ripping up my spine and out of the top of my head, *I'm on fire!* This rollercoaster of energy dominates me.

I am burning alive!
I can't catch my breath,
I have nothing left to scream with!

The burning sensation that courses through my body is so strange, and yet so familiar.

I think to myself, *Is my blood boiling in my veins? Am I being boiled alive?* At the same time, my body is floating on the bed.

Finally, I trust and surrender to the process.
I let the energy take over and I enjoy the ride.
That day, I let everything go on that table.

I understood; nothing was in my hands anymore.

As the class ended on that memorable third day, and everyone slowly left our sacred space, I rested in the stillness, not wanting to move.

Before I left, one of the teachers slipped a folded piece of paper into my hand. When I finally opened the paper, the words "Kundalini awakening" were scribbled on it.

I left the class, glad to see the sun as I walked home. *How did I get home? How did I unlock my door? Who put the clothes on my floor? What is a Kundalini awakening?*

**I went to bed feeling tired and happy.
I got another chance to live.**

I woke up in the middle of the night, terrified. I was experiencing the same energy that was present in class today, but now the energy came with a blinding white light. I was scared to be alone in my place with the thoughts in my mind.

*I am alone here.
I will die this time, and nobody will know.*

I surrendered to the experience and chose to face whatever shadows showed up.

I started to feel my body. *Am I dreaming? Am I in life? Am I dead?*

The experience had me questioning everything in life. I chose to get up and shift the energy. As I drank my water, my attention turned to the paper on my table that my teacher handed me. I started to research what a Kundalini awakening meant. I had never heard of it before. I found all the information which resonated with my experience but left me with even more questions.

The next day, I experienced a shift. I was no longer counting the days anymore, as I had let control go and enjoyed the energy I was receiving instead. Everyone wanted to know what happened and what I felt, but I had no words for them. I only wished for all of them to have the same experience I had.

I did not sleep for days, lost in my new little world.

On the last day of the course, we were asked to invite someone we could work on for the exam. I asked one of my friends to come and be my first victim. The massage was going well, when suddenly I noticed, all my teachers were in my room.

Why are you all here?
Is something going to happen?
The massage is almost over!

I asked my friend to flip over on her back, so I could work on her belly. I was overwhelmed with emotion, and I started to cry. Angel appeared beside me and put her hand on top of mine, pressing it into my friend's belly.

"Look at me. You can do it. You got this."
She steps back and I hear Angel's voice: *You can do it.*
I felt stronger and understood. *Yes, I can do it.*

I stopped crying, grounded myself, and the energy shifted.

My friend started to have an emotional release as I maintained the pressure on her belly. I stayed present with her, as that's what I needed when I went through the same thing earlier. I knew she was dealing with her stuff, and I knew I wouldn't leave her while she was doing it.

It didn't take long for her to surrender and trust the process. I could not believe I was experiencing my friend having an emotional release under my hands. I then realized you can control anything, no matter how strong (or not) you think you are.

She started to take a deep breath. "What happened? I don't remember," she questioned, dropping back into her body.

Holding her hand, I shared with her, "You were ready to let some things go." She felt light and happy after our session was over. "Thank you for being there for me, Emoke," she replied.

It was an intense experience to hold space and facilitate my first emotional release, while being assisted by Angel. I felt happy and strong, knowing I had someone who could step in and help.

Since that day, my life has shifted in amazing ways and different directions. I never thought I would be serving humanity the way I am today. The deep work I learned and experienced within that course helped me to see and understand more about the human body, energy, and emotional blockage.

This modality allowed me to gain deeper connections with a higher spirit, and the universe. Many thanks to my teachers for having the patience to help me understand how to trust my intuition. I appreciate them for pushing me through the leftover residual blockages and helping me start my new journey.

After completing the course, I felt the calling for my new life to start.

I started doing massages and a whole new world opened up for me. One surprise after another became my normal. I stepped into the flow of my new life. I still don't always understand what's happening through my touch, and what I'm able to do. I choose to follow my intuition and with pure intention, I know that I can trust it.

I started to be curious about energy work and did some Reiki courses to have more understanding of what I was doing. I always stayed connected with my teachers in case I had questions.

One day Angel and I decided to exchange a massage. She came to my space and while facilitating her massage I had a vision, a feeling. I felt the door open, and someone came into the room and stood by the door. As I was describing this presence, how it looked, what it was wearing, and what it was saying, she just listened.

"This is interesting," she replied. This spirit stayed there the whole time, as if it was assisting my job or holding space for her. As I was finishing, the spirit left. After the massage she pulled out her phone and showed me a person who was one of her mentors. Wow, she was exactly who I saw. "Isn't it interesting? I don't understand how that could happen!" I exclaimed.

"Emoke, not all humans with long hair are females," Angel replied.

What is happening? I do not understand!
How is this possible to see them? What do they want?
Why are they here?

"How far are you with your Reiki training?" Angel asked.

"I'm ready for my Master attunement, as I'm doing more than I have ever imagined. I'm ready!"

"Let's do it!"

The day came, and we made our way up the side of the dormant volcano at the edge of the city. Listening to the call of the sacred space, I found a ridge with a rock that could be used as a chair. I got comfortable and Angel started the ritual.

I found myself following the wind to my childhood graveyard in Transylvania.

I was participating in a ceremony with my relatives on Hallows Eve. I was visiting the deathbeds of my deceased relatives and celebrating them with prayer and candlelight, when I heard Angel calling my name.

As I dropped back into my body, I remember being surrounded by shamans, then an eagle eye came right to my face, to my eye, and blinked into my soul.

Angel translated what I did into words I understood. We shared deep conversations about what a channel is, and about tools to help us open our channel. We hold all the keys within.

She encouraged me to trust and keep going. "Do not be afraid and the right help will always show up when you need it."

I keep sharing my gifts and it gets easier to tune in and receive more guidance. The teachings were deep, and I went through a spiritual awakening during this process. I learned to let things go, and now I understand the benefits this work has for your health and body.

It is an amazing feeling to be able to help others on their own journey of transformation.

Finally, I understand: "When the student is ready the right teacher will show up."

The Medicine

We are taught how to be mad, resentful, and how to hold onto these negative emotions and other things that no longer serve us.

We hang onto people and experiences from long ago that don't exist in our worlds anymore. We have never been taught how to let things go.

Letting things go is not easy. It's a lot of work. It's our life's work; it never ends. But it's worth every minute when we decide we want to change our lives.

The medicine is in you. We can't change anything or anybody, except our own thoughts, patterns, and our view of life.

As soon as a trigger shows up, here are a few questions to ask yourself:

- What are you holding onto?
- Why are you holding onto it?
- Where do you feel the pain; is the pain familiar?
- Let all the answers come to you, experience them with emotion, and stay with yourself as you process the experience that shows up.
- Forgive yourself and the experience.
- Let it go! If you wait, it will be harder to do later.

You'll feel amazing the minute things shift and will want to continue doing it. As you start to teach your body, heart, and mind to let go, it gets easier.

You will want to see what's behind all the doors of your soul. You will want to clean out all that does not serve you, because you will begin to understand you do not need it. Waiting can have detrimental effects on your health.

From my own experience, the first breakthrough is the hardest. Then, you're gifted with the key to unlocking your heart and soul.

Experiencing true transformation, myself, I know how hard it is to let things go. We create different stories for the underlying issues that keep us stuck. People wait too long to release their pain. There is no point in holding anger, grief, or pain anymore.

Stop the addiction to suffering.

Most of us are never lucky enough to meet someone who can help us see and realize all the garbage we're carrying. I am grateful for the teachers who walked with me on my path and gave me the tools to now help others.

I'm encouraging you to be open and curious. Be open to change in your life and be willing to receive the help you deserve. I know the usual is so convenient, even if it's painful, because the unknown is so scary. But are you really happy with the life you have right now?

As soon as you are ready for the unknown, it will show itself to you, and it is beautiful.

Emoke is a skilled massage and bodywork practitioner from the Raynor Naturopathic School of Massage and Bodywork. Her work with Angel has allowed her the honor of being one of the first Priestess initiates of the Nina Songo Energy Medicine Mystery School and Reiki Master through the Usui System of Natural Healing.

In her free time, you can find her climbing mountains, swimming in lakes and creating magical herbal medicine in her kitchen.

Connect with Emoke at:

Email: mocike13@gmail.com

Facebook: https://www.facebook.com/emoke.molnar.583

"The medicine is in you. We can't change anything or anybody, except our own thoughts, patterns, and our view of life."

~ Emoke Molnar

CHAPTER 16

SADDLING THE HEART

A JOURNEY BACK THROUGH THE SOUL

Dustin Kaiser

My Story

Most of this life, I rode alone.
From high desert mountains to the valleys below,
through the depths of my heart and the shadows of my past,
I rode through life way too fast.
Not paying attention to things as they come,
reaching for alcohol to help me feel numb.
I relied on a bottle to hide behind my heart,
a drink or two every night so my feelings would not start.
I was a tough cowboy I played the part,
riding wild horses from dawn till dark.
Pushing cattle to places they didn't want to go,
This is how I used to feed my wild soul.

I tip my hat to shield my face from the freezing northern wind as the snow pushes across my rose-colored cheeks. I kick my horse into a trot trying to get to the shelter sooner. I try to keep a perfect cadence, so he does not lose his footing and slip on the ice-covered desert floor. I swung my leg over the saddle, stepping off of my horse to fix the broken fence. My boots sank down into the freshly fallen snow. Suddenly, I find myself dropping to my knees, tears flowing from my eyes, as flashbacks from my four-wheeler accident came barreling through me like a motion picture. This was the moment I died at age 18, when I met my Creator and was given a choice.

Am I going to fulfill my life's purpose?
Am I going to start over again?
Is it time for me to let go and start a new life cycle?
I want to stay on Earth. I know I can be happy here.
I choose to stay.
I set my soul on fire.

I open my heart to let it all go, I opened
my hands to guide me to the light.

Help me Lord, this cowboy has no more fight.

The messages echoed through my soul from the different teachers who came to me from my past, guiding and holding me in love. Then, like a crack of thunder from up above;

This is the day I let it all go;
this is the day I bury it in the cold winter snow.
This will be your Ego's last ride.

I'm here today writing this chapter, hoping this gives you the courage, heart, and guidance to follow your soul's true purpose. It was a rough road for this cowboy. I battled right out of high school with depression and suicide, alcohol addiction, married and divorced with a DUI before I was 21 years old.

I had enough! I knew I must turn my life around. I loaded up my saddle, and headed for Nevada to cowboy on the big ranches and figure out this life purpose I was supposed to learn. The next few years I traveled from ranch to ranch through Nevada, and up through Montana chasing greener grass, bigger pastures, and new mountains to ride, trying to find something to keep me alive, buried in a bottle of booze keeping me from feeling my feelings. Alcohol was the only thing that made me think I fit in with the other cowboys. I knew in the depths of my soul that I was here for something bigger.

Why would I get a second chance?
I sure as hell was not meant to be a whiskey-drunk, saddle tramp.

I've always practiced saying yes to an opportunity to face the unknown. It's one of my greatest thrills. That's how I ended up in northern British Columbia. That's where I met my first teacher, a local elder from the tribe up north who showed up at the ranch where I was working that day. The moment he got out of his truck, our souls connected as we talked about hunting. Little did I know, the thing he was hunting was my own soul.

Who is this guy? He feels so familiar.

I knew in my heart that he was there to help me. "Would you be interested in me doing some healing work on you?" he offered. Without hesitation, I said, "Yes!"

As he placed his hands on my bare chest, I could smell the Palo Santo he burned. This was something so new to me, but so familiar. Something I've smelled my entire life, but I've never heard of. He moved energy and worked on my eyes. Opening up my heart chakra, he removed ancestral blockages. It was one of the most amazing experiences I've ever felt in my life. Our session started to come to a close, and I fluttered to open my eyes. I could see him lean over me, with his hands on my chest, sweat running down his face, with a big grin, looking into my soul. He told me, "You know that you're supposed to be doing this, right?"

With a big sheepish grin and no words on my lips, my heart answered the call. I didn't even have a clue what 'this' was. I knew how to ride broncs and push cows; that is what I knew. This new energy poured through every part of my body. Just like Palo Santo, so strange but so familiar. This ignited a fire deep in my soul, and I wanted to dive in for more!

I was lucky enough to work with him often throughout the summer before I went back down to the states. I couldn't handle the frozen northern country anymore, so I headed to California which was a hell of a lot warmer.

California is where I met the love of my life.
A beautiful blonde cowgirl that someday, I would call my wife.
Little did I know this cowgirl would play a part,
in the settling of my wild heart.

Our summer started off in love,
with many nights staring at the stars above.
Speaking of dreams and manifestation,
talking about silly cowboy meditations.

Summer came and summer went, that fall I got into a wreck.
Shattered my leg from my knee to my toes,
this is where opportunity arose.

April found a therapy called Bowen two years prior,
she'd already been goin'.
It helped her with her muscles, it helped to stay on track.
It kept her moving forward, from horse wrecks a while back.

It came to me one night in the dream,
it came to me like it was meant to be.
When the words "Learn Bowen" echoed through my soul!
This is where my medicine would grow.
I followed the schooling through and through,
finishing what I started like cowboys do.
Letting my hands guide the way,
I had no clue where this would take me someday.

As the grass started to grow, it was time for us to go.
We moved to Oregon, this is where my deep healing really began.

I took a job at a high mountain ranch.
Living that far from town will sure give a cowboy a chance,
to sit in the evenings and talk about cowboy romance.

Now cowboy romance you see, it's not what you might think it to be.
I'm not talking about a night on the town,
I'm talking about sitting with your feelings when no one's around.
Sitting on top of an icy ridge waiting for the sun to rise
will sure give a cowboy time to sit and think and feel wise.

Watching the deer in the meadows below,
who else can sit atop and horse and get their chakras to glow!
Now these are things I used to keep to myself,
for I didn't need the other cowboys getting roused.
So you see, talking romance was different for me.

April would give me the chance that I need,
to walk in our house, to sing and to dance.
She would hold the space for me, she gave me the chance to just be. . .

We would speak of things so deep and so true,
we would share pieces of medicine that we both knew.
Chakras, stones and sticks, moving energy with the flick of the wrist.
Healing our traumas we would share from our past,
releasing the things that no longer last.
We are twin flames that have finally crossed paths.

The more time we spent together, the more we did shift.
As we both continue to walk into our own special gifts.

Summer had come and winter went,
it was time for us to travel living out of our cowboy tent.
Looking for new work to do, something cowboys are accustomed to.
But this time was different you see, this time I had a partner with me.

We had a lot of fun that summer, traveling from ranch to ranch.
Trying to find that special place where we could hang our hats.

We traveled through Tehachapi,
then over to Nevada across that Sagebrush Sea.
Checked out a ranch near Salt Lake City,
there were too many people for me.
None of those ranches made our heart dance,
so we packed up our saddles giving Oregon another chance.

As it started to get cold and I came to my senses,
I finally realized I was done riding these old damn fences.
As I picked up myself from the snow covered floor,
I knew I would not be riding these broncs anymore.
I climbed on my horse and straddled my saddle,
trotting back home, to tell my wife about this epic battle.
As we laid in bed later that evening,
I put down the book that I had been reading.
I told her what happened that day, I told her that it would all be okay!
She looked at me with a great big grin and said,
"This is where your medicine begins."

The Medicine

When we begin our walks through our inner journeys, this can be a very dark and lonely time of releasing and surrendering, but as we continue to walk through this path and work through our shadows, the reward on the other side is pure bliss—you start to align with your soul's true purpose. Here are some helpful tools I've picked up along the way.

ALLOW YOURSELF TO DIE

This is the moment when you hit that breaking point that can be referred to as rock bottom. When you're in that space and decide to make a change, one thing you can do is sit down and make a list of five things you want to rebirth in your new life. Examples are love, abundance, health, spirituality, well-being, commitment, or whatever your heart may desire. Write these things down somewhere where you can see them daily so you can start creating that new story of rebirthing your new life.

RELEASE EVERYTHING

One way to practice this is to write a letter to all the people or things that have got you to the point where you are today. The point of releasing and falling back in love with yourself. This letter is to take your power back! You can be as aggressive or meaningful as you need to be. Remember, the point of this is to let it all go! Then burn it. Hold yourself in a sacred ceremony while releasing all the things written in this letter that are no longer part of your story.

SURRENDER

Surrender to yourself. Sit with yourself alone. Take time to accept that sometimes life is unfair. Sometimes life is painful and overwhelming. Take time to be honest with yourself. Start dealing with your own emotions. You can't run from them and you can't avoid them any longer. It's time to surrender to yourself. Love yourself and who you truly are!

DROP YOUR EGO

This can be a very hard thing as we move forward in our journeys. Sometimes our ego is our identity. It's who we have created but does not align with our true divine selves. Here are a few ways to help you drop your ego and connect with your divine soul purpose:

Be in a state of openness. You can't learn if you think you already know.

Release your pride. It's okay to need others. Be open to love and acceptance of abundance.

Connect with nature. Take off your boots and connect to Mother Earth. Tell her all of the things you're ready to release, and let her take that energy that no longer serves you.

Start loving yourself. Listen to yourself and fall back in love with the things that help you to make your medicine. Make time to take care of yourself.

One other thing that can be a very powerful tool through this journey of releasing things, is to write your own eulogy. Sit down and talk with yourself. You will find the things that truly matter in your life when you decide to let it all go.

Because with every death comes rebirth; this is our time to shine! As we have no more attachments to the things that never mattered in the first place. We are in line with our true divine selves. Loving ourselves and others can be the greatest medicine of all.

A near death experience combined with the bumps, bruises, and broken bones that come from a lifetime of long days in the saddle tending to cattle and training young horses, **Dustin** was guided into alternative medicine in search of living a pain free and natural lifestyle. Diving deep into the spiritual well-being and the retrieval of his own soul. Opening his heart to help others experience the same opportunities, Buckaroo Buddha Holistic Healing LLC was established in 2019, by April and Dustin Kaiser. Building a bridge for the ranching community and those alike providing physical, mental, and spiritual well-being. Peace, Health, and Cowboy Shit.

- Bowen Therapy Specialist
- Shamanic Master Reiki Energy Healing and Ceremony
- Soul Retrieval
- Activation Breathwork

Connect with Dustin Kaiser:

Email address:
buckaroobuddha1111@gmail.com

Website:
https://www.buckaroobuddha.com

Linkedin:
https://www.linkedin.com/in/buckaroo-buddha-4137a2232/

Facebook:
https://www.facebook.com/buckaroobuddha1111

Instagram:
https://www.instagram.com/buckaroobuddha1111/

"A spiritual journey is like riding a fresh colt. Sometimes you're going to get your guts stomped on. But as you progress through your journey you learn to ride with presence, perfect cadence and flow."
Life: Take a deep seat.

~ Dustin Kaiser

CHAPTER 17

THE ENLIGHTENED LEADERSHIP

LEADERS ARE NOT MADE
BUT UNVEILED

Gurpreet Juneja

My Story

It's time to move on and find something else; it's not working out the way I want it to; with a deep sigh, I leave the room. As I walked towards the car in the parking lot, my cell phone ringtone startled me, snapping me into the present time. "Hey Paul, did you pick her up yet? I'm running late," I uttered.

"Yes, she's with me, so take your time; no rush," Paul assured me.

The next 53 minutes going down Highway 36, tested my car driving efficiency to get home faster. I could only think about which turns to take to get home and be with my 18-month-old baby; I couldn't wait to see the joy in her eyes.

I feel the separation from her, and it kills me not to be with her in these young years of her life when she needs my love and care the most. But I am also committed to my success, my career, and making a difference in the world; why can't I balance? Why can't I do both and dance between the two happily and willingly?

A little face peeked through the garage door, screaming, "Mama is home, Mama is home," as I parked my car. Holding her in my arms, I felt alive again, living and breathing.

"I should get some dinner ready for us," I whispered to my child, Khushie.

"Mommy, I want you to build Legos with me, please," she insisted. Feeling torn, I explained how being late from work today would cause a further delay in the whole schedule.

"What do you want to build today, sweet pea?" I asked.

"I want to make a house," she giggles.

"Hmm. I don't know how to make a house. How about you start, and I will join?" Can I convince her she could play while I watched her from the kitchen so we all could eat on time? Of course, she builds and breaks different structures as I make lentil soup with mixed vegetable stir fry. I know what I did there, and it hurts.

"It's time for dinner; let's check if Papa is off his work calls."

Dinner times are the only times I can sit.

Before I settled on that thought: "Mama, can you take me potty, please?" I hear. That's the norm; the dinner table reminds Khushie her tummy is full and needs to be emptied before putting in more food. Staring at the clock, I work with my little one practicing her potty training skills, not forgetting about the 30-second hand washing routine I reinforce until it becomes her second nature.

Hopefully, the Indian spice smell all over the house made her hungry enough to return and have dinner before it got too cold, I wish.

"It's too spicy, Mama. I'm not hungry. I want to play," Khushie exclaimed, climbing up to the dining table.

I barely get a couple of hours with her. Do I spend it disciplining her, feeding her, teaching her all the necessary life skills, or just be loving and play? I'm still figuring out that balance. This is my first child. I must give myself some grace.

"Baby, we'll play only after dinner. The sooner you eat, the more play time we have, it's already 7:30 p.m., and your bedtime is at 8:30 p.m. Let's move faster," I lovingly say.

Khushie picked and ate only the peas and a quarter of an Indian roti (bread). It took her about 30 minutes to wrap up dinner. *How do I tell her I must shower and get her ready for bed, which means there is no time to play? Ugh, she is not going to like it.*

"Time to play, Mama," she says with excitement.

"How about we play in the shower with water?" I say, trying to convince her to shower.

"But you said we'll play after dinner," she frowns at me, crossing her arms and stomping her tiny little feet.

"I know, but we also must watch the time and make sure you get lots of dreams in the night, playing and having fun with the new friends you're making at school," I state, kissing her.

With her head down, she walks towards the shower. Trying to control her giggles as I tickle her, she pretends to be mad at me for consistently not doing what she wants me to do.

Getting to bed is no less than a battle of love because she wants me to sleep with her, whereas, as a good mother, I should teach her to sleep by herself. The most adorable stories of *Winnie the Pooh* not letting her sleep in her bed alone melt my heart. Gosh, parenting is challenging and painful, yet so rewarding. It's almost 9:00 p.m. by the time I see her sound asleep.

As I prepare for the following day, I hear Paul's footsteps approaching.

"How was your day, today?" he asks. "Did Greg say anything today?" With a pause, he looked at me with curious eyes.

"Greg put me on probation," I said with an increased heart rate as I talked.

"Probation, for what?" Paul asked. "You're so dedicated and sincere, and you even brought such a good name to them," he remembered.

Crossing my arms with a sharp tone, I said, "Well, somehow, I have not been able to keep up with the eight-to-five routine and leave a little early every day."

"Babe, I don't want you to worry about picking up Khushie from her preschool every day after work. It's okay; I will take care of her," Paul assured me.

Drawing my breath and releasing it with force, I felt my face getting hot. "Don't you think Greg needs to understand that if I get all my work done and am productive, it shouldn't be a big deal to leave work 20-30 minutes early? Because her preschool closes at five, I must get there to pick her up and take her home, and it's a long time for her to be in that daycare eight-to-five. I get in the office around 8:00-8:15 a.m. I don't even use my lunch hour. Based on university policy, all employees must stay eight to five. I don't get it. I don't understand what the big deal is. And clearly, he doesn't want to understand. And why would he? He doesn't have any children; what would he know what it takes to raise them?" I said, crossing my arms in frustration.

"I know you're annoyed and angry, it's not an easy job to be a mother of a young child and be working, but we must find a balance to make sure nothing gets hurt; I can drive up to Boulder from Broomfield and get to her preschool in 20-25 minutes, pick her up, and head home." With confidence, Paul nodded his head.

"How logical is that? We put her in daycare next to me so I can drop her off and pick her up, and I'm closer to her if need be. And then there are times when you are traveling out of the city; I thought that was why we found a preschool for her in Boulder. Or am I missing something?" I pounded a fist against the kitchen island.

"Well, I'm only trying to help; getting irritated at me will not solve our problem. But I suggest I pick her up on regular days unless I'm not in town. You do pickups on days I can't, and since that's not too many days, you might be able to get an exception to get out early for those days when I'm not here. So instead of getting frustrated, tell Greg that tomorrow, he may re-think the probation," Paul said, continuing to be deliberate with his calm voice.

"I don't think he will re-think; he is making his boss, Vik Goldberg, hand over the probation documents to me and sign them. Can you believe that? Don't forget this guy applauded me for developing the Equation Editor tool, a unique offering in the Campus Solution environment. This tool automated the grand scan amount for students applying for financial aid. It was not yet thought of until now. I presented the tool at the HEUG (Higher Education Users Group) conference earlier this year. After the word got out, many universities contacted us to leverage the tool."

I have a creative mindset, but to tap into the creativity, they must be open to being flexible with the life changes we employees deal with as we raise a family. The rules in the workforce are not designed for women and especially a mother. It's time for me to move on. It's unfortunate; how much I suffocate my love for my child to feel worthy of making my dream come true, feeling betrayed and judged for not being able to stay in the office till 5:00 p.m.

Walking towards the refrigerator, I continued to reflect.

Mornings are always chaotic with our 18-month-old child. She wants to share all her imaginative stories, and I mostly rush to get out the door with her to make it on time. The smell of the burnt toast and spilled milk mess all over the kitchen table would rush Paul to salvage breakfast.

There was nothing wrong with any of us; she is a child. She's going to spill the milk and make a mess, which is how she learns how not to. But when do I give her time to be herself and learn these lessons at her own pace?

I can feel my nervousness building as I deal with being late another day.

I gave it my all but did not get support and understanding when I needed it. I'm losing respect for this institution for what it's worth; they killed my creativity and my dedication to the mission of this company.

My mind raced, while driving down Highway 36 to work.

"Have a seat, Gurpreet," Vic said. "It's always tough to talk about stuff like this, but we will put you on probation for six months, hoping you'll change your patterns of arriving late or leaving early from work. If this behavior doesn't change, then you will be asked to leave the organization." Vic's accusing words pierced my eardrums.

With a dry mouth and throbbing head, I spoke up. "But Vic, I'm only late by a few minutes. Sometimes I get here at 8:10, 8:15 at the latest, and then I leave around 4:45 to pick up my kiddo, who's not too far from here. With the traffic time, it takes me 10-12 mins to get to her. Her preschool closes at 5. I must pick her up then," I explained as if I was on a witness stand, trying to explain why I committed the crime of being late or leaving early.

"I understand, but this organization requires people at work for nine hours, including lunch, and your manager specifically wants you to be at your desk for this time. He is here from 7-5 and sometimes even longer. You must follow your manager's policy, which aligns with the organization's policy," Vic clarifies sternly.

"All I'm asking for is some grace; the work period is eight hours, equating to 40 hours a week. I'm already doing that; I don't take lunch breaks at all; I think that one hour of lunch is something I could use as a window to make things work for my personal life."

I didn't drop to my knees at this point.

"Understood, but as per your manager, every individual needs an hour of lunchtime to be productive for the rest of the day; it's their choice how they spend it. In your case, you work, but that is not the expectation; instead, the expectation is to be in the office nine hours." He wouldn't budge.

It was clear, Vic was not listening at this point; glancing at the paperwork and at the clock, he handed me the paperwork with assertiveness. "You need to sign this paper that you accept you will be on probation, and you will have six months to change your pattern of being tardy at work."

Are you serious? You will not listen to me despite the caliber I have shown you. If you give me what I am asking for, I will provide you with my best. Why is it so much about the hours rather than showing up to work with the right mindset? Will I be productive these next six months when I know somebody will watch the clock over my shoulder?

In my career of over 20 years being a leader, as I hired people and worked with different teams, I realized that leadership is about understanding your people, their mindset, and creating a synergy between these people is the essence of successful leadership. As a thoughtful leader I comprehended, just like a gardener never forces her will on the plants but instead just dances around the needs of the plants, for them to shine their unique abilities, similarly, if I can understand the goals, lifestyle, and priorities of my people then I give them room to create their own magic while we all dance with what works best for everyone creating a momentum of joy and fulfillment, making us all successful. I have been using this medicine ever since then and it has never failed me but always surprised me with how powerful it can be to empower our people.

The Medicine

THE GARDENER MEDICINE

A leader is like a gardener, responsible for the well-being of all different plants and shrubs in their garden. Leadership is not about telling people what to do but inspiring them to be unique. Every plant requires a fantastic array of necessities to survive and thrive. We all are unique in every way. Our fingerprints don't match, and neither does our DNA. How can we all think the same and be the most productive beings in the same environment? We can't. We all need our environment to shine our light and share it with the world, bringing out our best. The plant or the shrub will only shine its beauty fully if given the right resources, time, and a healthy environment to grow to its potential.

Leading is the most humbling experience, giving you a platform to nurture a garden full of talents and expertise. Your job as a leader is to get out of the way and let these talents and expertise shine and intertwine for the most beautiful and unique permutations to emerge. My struggles with being successful in my career without authentic, heartfelt leadership gave me insights into what thoughtful leadership should look like:

1. Authenticity over Perfection

Everybody's a leader since we all learn to lead our lives, but a true leader comes from a place of authenticity rather than righteousness. Being right is a relative term; something right in my eye could be offensive to someone else. But when you're authentic, you share your thoughts behind a decision. When planting, a gardener could misjudge the plant's place in his garden, which might lead to a misfit. Having a clear understanding, acknowledging, and authenticity of matching your actions with your intentions to change the environment for the betterment of the plant is the only way to salvation. A thoughtful leader knows being authentic makes you vulnerable, but that's being human. When you're disingenuous and helpless as a leader, you also set the team's tone.

2. Connection over Competition

Competition is essential; it builds grit and resilience, but becomes selfish and demeaning when competition faces outward. A plant competes with the environment to grow and nurture itself if provided with all the essentials to live. People should learn to compete with themselves and be better than yesterday, rather than competing with another human or teammate for a project or promotion. Competition is healthy between two exact things, apples and apples, not apples and oranges. In most cases, teammates compete when they need to share skill sets, goals, or job responsibilities. On the other hand, connection to their proper source helps people find their passion and build on their strengths, sharing their knowledge and expertise with people around them, just like a plant shares a flower or a fruit.

3. Empathy over Directive

The gardener doesn't judge the plants that need more water or resources than others; as a caretaker, he offers all needed for their growth. As a manager, I noticed the more understanding I became and started seeing the view from the other side, the more productive and committed my team became. As leaders, we must remember that our most valuable resource is our people. The more we connect with them, the more we learn about each other, leading to growth. That doesn't mean we work with something unacceptable, but again connection teaches you how to tackle challenging situations, which is growth. The ruling leadership approach kills thinking. And we pay people for their thinking.

4. Process over Progress

Enhancing the expected performance of the employee is a key to successful leadership, but before that comes the clarity of the path, which is the process. As a gardener, planning all the steps necessary for the plant to flourish, setting clear expectations and milestones, and triggering a creative, thoughtful mindset with positive feedback is core to being a successful leader.

5. Leading from Behind over Leading from the Front

Rather than showing your team how to do things a certain way, a leader needs to inspire others to do their own thinking. That's why they're part of the team, to provide innovative solutions with their thought processes. A gardener never forces or shows the plant how to absorb the sunlight or other nutrients from the soil; they provide all that's needed and trust the plant to do its magic. Leading from behind helps people build self-esteem and confidence and inspires them to make informed decisions. Don't get me wrong, leading from the front is also needed, but for situations where your organization might be going through a change. The leader should lead by example, jumping in first to adapt themselves to the change. Leading from behind and front should usually follow the 80:20 rule.

6. Stability over Variability

The work environment brings a lot of uncertainty with changing requirements and deliverables. When changing weather crumbles the plant, the gardener's undivided dedication to nurturing every environment creates a balance for the plant to survive. Similarly, providing stable leadership, with the meaning of "I got your back no matter what," creates homeostasis in people and does not push them into their survival instincts, moving them into fight or flight mode, which kills not only creativity but also clogs the thought process.

Based on the type of plant in the garden, the appropriate ecosystem is stipulated for it to survive. Just like no two plants are the same, no two employees are the same. Everybody needs their environment to strive and thrive in. Bringing that creativity forth and thinking like a gardener switches a leader into a caretaker mindset fostering a healthy, well-maintained blossoming garden full of fruitful and luscious plants and shrubs.

Gurpreet Kaur Juneja is an emotion and energy healer, holistic life coach, speaker, author, and certified NeuroChangeSolutions consultant. She supports young people, men, women, and parents challenged by life, and living under stress feeling burnt out. She provides both in-person and virtual, individual and group healing and coaching services.

Under her business BeingCosmo, she also offers webinars, podcasts and hosts a variety of healthy and happy lifestyle workshops providing hands-on tools for true transformation from the inside out. The 'cosmo' echoes the unlimited being we are, containing the wisdom of the Universe within ourselves. It is also a reminder of our oneness with everything around us.

Gurpreet channels divine essence and can help people connect. Her vision is to help everyone connect with their soul, the divine within, and seed unconditional love for all on this beautiful Gaia.

As a wife and mother and with over 20 years of leadership experience in tech space, Gurpreet has found true joy, peace, and ecstasy in her path of life by following the divine energy found in her heart and wants to kindle this fire in every heart, helping others tap into their own true essence.

Constantly challenging her own potential, as an agent of change she is focused on inspiring people to maximize their personal and professional potential and provokes her clients to think outside the box, widen their imagination and expectation from themselves, helping them go beyond their limited selves.

Gurpreet's soul sings when connecting to Mother Earth. When she's not working, you'll find her hiking or driving the glorious sunny mountains, meditating under the dark sky, or immersed in cooking something full of life made with fresh veggies she planted in her own backyard.

Connect with Gurpreet:

Website: www.beingcosmo.com; www.cosmobeing.com

Facebook: https://www.facebook.com/iamacosmobeing

Instagram: https://www.instagram.com/cosmo_being

LinkedIn: https://www.linkedin.com/company/iamacosmobeing

"We all lead in some fashion or form, but leading from our hearts is where our true power is, not just for us but for others to find their real strengths connecting us at a much deeper level."

~ Gurpreet Juneja

CHAPTER 18

RIDING THROUGH THE FIRE

A COCOON'S JOURNEY IN SEARCH OF HEAVEN ON EARTH

April Kaiser

My Story

The ways in which my ancestors set me up to gallop through fires in their own unique and private way, is the gratitude I hold in every ceremony today. Magical helpers were dotted throughout my younger years as breadcrumbs on my journey to awareness. Looking back now, I'm able to see, for example, how my grandmother played an important role in the protection of my birth. She helped cure the spiritual glitch we're both aware of, and has now taken from me the cross that I bear, breaking a generational curse.

My aunt completed her part, communicating with me and expressing in great detail how this glitch came to be. This confirmation validated my experience and fortified my path forward. An adopted mother gave me the tools to survive in this life, deepening my warrior goddess. My grandfather appeared through a psychic gypsy healer expressing to me the importance of severing every single one of my relationships. These are some of the huge clues along my personal path that I've held onto for continued medicine.

Humans are domesticated by control. Control is what holds us in cages of thoughts fed to us by authority. Often, we don't attempt to question out of fear of punishment, such as removing personal rights to free will.

This may sound severe to some, but others will know what I'm speaking of. These things were made very clear to me as a young child raised in an authoritative family, within an extreme religious organization. Guilt is one tool used to gain more control. "If you were to leave God's one and only true religion, your example would turn others away. Therefore, every single person you're ever in contact with (past, present, and future) will not receive eternal salvation and it will be all your fault. You're taking everyone to Hell with you, and that's so much worse. Don't be selfish!"

When people are put in this type of cage it's impossible to see through a window of open mindedness, let alone hold faith in any sort of real present life, past lives, other people, spirituality, or the love that exists.

Since these vibrations came from people outside of our religion, they were considered foreign entities and weren't welcome in our households' soul space. Presence, past life understandings and so much more were not of our faith, and therefore, wouldn't be with our religion. Riding through this fire wounds the child's heart. The true family I felt most connected to, my blood family that truly loved us, weren't good enough by certain standards and were therefore banned because of one-sided religious beliefs. I was forced to abide in a tribe full-time that felt completely foreign to me.

Tapping into mechanisms for salvation as a young child, such as empathy or an open mind and heart, were all against the rules. When domesticated beliefs become our thoughts and feelings, the sense of deep responsibilities and our core beliefs take their toll emotionally, mentally, spiritually, and physically, to the point of death. This place of the first death is also the same place where we may begin to see the possibility of having a one-on-one relationship with Source, our Creator. This space is where the clues on what should be done next live.

Aligning with an open mind and an open heart is part of it—allowing the personal relationship with God to play out without interruption from any egoistic outside forces. Caged thoughts and feelings from these outside forces certainly bring unhappiness to all animals. Finding gratitude within the cocoon will break the seal on this cage that many of us are or were trapped inside of. The more things we can possibly be grateful for, the sooner the doors of freedom will burst open and disintegrate into nothing.

Early on, I learned to survive on gratitude. Despite the heavy curse I carried on this tiny little girl's shoulders, I felt privileged to be raised on a working ranch. Ranch related chores, church meetings, studying, and public school consumed my time. I worked even harder to realize the ecstasy of the moment of the freedom to ride. Exploring with our ranch horses deep in the forest helped me lose myself in the semblance of a perceived childhood.

At one point, a family friend gave me her beloved horse. She was a jet-black thoroughbred, which was the first big animal medicine presented to me. My horse journey began as Atman came in the form of my adopted mother (who was not affiliated with our church) passing down her ways to me. Being surrounded by four older brothers who taught me the cowboy ways did not leave much room for the tenderness of the feminine. I was gifted with the much needed soft hands for my new gorgeous and perfect horse, balancing the masculine and feminine. She gave me the gift of true horsemanship that surpassed what most were accustomed to, truly saving my life.

I never dismounted, and went on professionally training countless horses for the next 35 years. Every day and every night, I was on horseback looking for moments of bliss. There is a special place of firmness, yet surrendering to humility when you're on horseback. With lots of love and time put into training, reaching a neutral point with this amazing spirit, partnered up, taps into Heaven in many ways. It's a very desirable place to be. This is the only thing on Earth that kept me here.

I rode through the fire of suicide, internal heartbreak, and the renunciation of parents with an entire known tribe as I left the church and the only belief system I knew, jumping out of one frying pan into another, experiencing years of trauma with no support. I now see how important all of this was as part of my tiger journey, consistently on the hunt for truth. I hunted for a way to see the universe shift what was out of my control.

Riding wild horses, I left the toxic safety of the church, entering another hell. Working with soul contracts, sorrow, and pain, I embarked on a 20-year partnership of sweat, blood, dirt, and broken bones. The new tribe I was surrounded by excelled in textbook narcissism, mixed with narcotic and alcohol abuse. During this time, I rode through the fire of the cocoon, spiritually awakening through a broken neck and jaw injuries. While I now live in 'aliveness,' I still have lifelong chronic syndromes because of these events. Out of a grave that came with this first death, I saw that I must evolve or repeat the past. Identifying the pain body, it was time to heal my broken bones and process the things I'd been spiritually downloading. Being still and gaining inner power, yet physically healing through multiple surgeries caused me to come out as an even stronger warrior. Dragonfly enters my everyday life to hold me close as an angel, bringing me patience and stillness, along with toughness, since they've existed for over 3,000 years. Dragonfly teaches me (again) to balance the masculine and feminine parts of my character.

At this time, digging deep into the way of the Toltec, which is certainly the medicine to be seeking for anyone with caged thoughts, I came across the simplicity of their explanation of Heaven on Earth and how it's accessible to us personally at any time during our lifetime. I knew from personal experience we were living in Hell. Yet this way allowed me to explore as if I could see the magic switch within my reach, using gratitude as the tool to flip it in search of Heaven on Earth during this lifetime.

Riding through this new fire, I was determined to heal myself, cut all cords with toxic and unhealthy baggage, dedicate myself to the Creator and experience what we speak of. Breaking away from my career and the only thing I knew, unable to physically ride horses again, I set out in search of what Source would provide.

Through acceptance, things began to shift and I saw what I deserved for all of my pure faith and hard work. I would manifest and create my own life from here on, consistently encouraging transition into my higher self, balancing the masculine and feminine I carry, and using gratitude as my main life tool. I would be thankful for every possible thing I saw rather than the negative illusion of the circumstances. I thirsted to create the life I felt would get me further down the enlightened road.

Before I knew it, just like a light switch, Heaven appeared within me day after day as I literally packed up my horses, work dogs, and child, taking off into the wilderness where we'd heal. I'm a pure cowboy, so I'd never imagined a 'knight in shining armor.' Once I healed myself, my twin flame came fast as a shaman buckaroo, healing me in every way left possible. Together we created Heaven on Earth daily in true form.

The Medicine

Finding your own medicine may have already come or you may feel like that concept is far away. Your medicine is a gift for the better of humanity, and it makes your soul shine, plain and simple. That is what the saying means when referring to 'your life's purpose.' If you know what is for you, ride for it like no other! Every speed bump is worth all of the effort to live your life in a heavenly state. If you're too exhausted for now, receive and gather what works for you in your personal basket of tools to get through your awakening. Maybe someday you will share it. Ride through the fire and you'll gain strength.

When you're at your best, express gratitude. When you're at your worst, express gratitude. Thankfulness in any form will shift the vibrations of your circumstances to what's best for your highest good.

I remember waking up from my neck surgery, unable to move any muscle in my entire body because it was on lockdown. I started by counting the holes in the tile of the hospital ceiling, thankful that my voice box was okay. Gratefulness will always work as a personal shovel if you're in any sort of hole. Continuing this practice at all times is part of your medicine. How far you take this medicine of gratitude is how much you'll be grateful for. It'll bring awareness to your life and with that, we learn to balance the masculine and feminine in a way that serves our highest good.

Accepting help from the outside can be a good idea, when presented in alignment with your journey, filling your soul with peace and happiness.

The tribe you can trust from outside of your cocoon are people with no ego. You'll have to ride through some fire, but they will safely hold space for your path of self-healing in search of your Heaven on Earth.

Chakra healing will ignite other important resources for your medicine basket. Reaching out to angels and your animal guides who come to us in forms we can accept, relying on their messages to show you the way that's best for your path.

My adopted mother and I met on the battlefield three years ago, when she summoned me to administer her death with dignity juice into her hands. Another fire to ride through! We were now full circle. She saved my life, and I saved hers. I've been rewarded fully. Today I live with Black Jaguar Medicine, soaking up what I can from what it has to offer. I've received clarity, that solitude and observation are key forms of medicine to my survival right now. Breathwork Ceremony has opened all of the doors with the answers I've ever searched for. I spend quality time with her as 'Atman,' the most beautiful white horse with a black mane and tail. I've been searching for this white horse around every waking corner for the last eight years since a shaman expressed that I would, "See it as a sign of my confirmation." She comes to me with healing, clarity, and messages, guiding me on how to open my heart and be love. She and this Jaguar race down the coastline of the jungle, neck and neck in my journey, although she laughs at the idea of me ever winning. Most of my healing tools, such as rattle and drum are made from horsehide to facilitate my clients' journeys.

Once you've healed yourself and have raised the bar on who has access to your energy, you may also find yourself in a place to heal others in some ways from your basket. Turning hurt into compassion is the highest form of magic in human form. It sounds easy, but it's a ride through fire. Just like me writing this chapter for others, I hope your hurt can transform into compassion somehow as well.

MY LOVE LETTER TO YOU

"I am grateful that you've opened yourself up and are searching for what your soul seeks. Be aware that it takes time to process and heal. My prayer for you is that you just don't hold back! Don't let anyone manipulate and force their spiritual beliefs, or even simple things such as what you should eat for dinner, onto you. You are here with your own identity and God-given intuitions. Own them and be proud of what your Creator has given you, remembering your birthright of free will. With time so valuable, stop sitting in anything not meant for you. Shine your bright light. It's actually a lot easier than you think!

I'll be here for you in your time of need, riding through fire. Speeding towards the day we rejoice, riding even harder and faster through the High Sierra meadows, full of blue forget-me-not flowers, with our arms straight out to our sides and our heads thrown back in the wind, in Heaven on Earth, here and now. I'll now be packing our picnic lunch in a saddlebag for us to share out there. It must be created!"

As a lifelong rancher and professional horse trainer living day-to-day with chronic repercussions from serious injuries, April reached out to alternative medicine in search of living a pain free and natural lifestyle. Feeling the call to help others experience the same opportunities, Buckaroo Buddha Holistic Healing LLC was established in 2019, by April and Dustin Kaiser. Building a Bridge for the ranching community and those alike providing physical, mental, and spiritual well-being. Peace, health, and cowboy shit.

- Bowen Therapy Specialist
- Reiki Energy Healing and Ceremony
- Shamanic Practitioner
- Buckaroo Buddha Breathwork Facilitator
- Member of Brave Badass Healers Community - working closely with religious trauma and your spiritual awakening, narcissism abuse support, cord cutting, and removing attachments. She shares her authentic journey, cowboy logic and straightforwardness, creating a path aligned with your soul's journey and highest good.

Connect with April Kaiser:

Email address:
buckaroobuddha1111@gmail.com

Website:
https://www.buckaroobuddha.com

Linkedin:
https://www.linkedin.com/in/buckaroo-buddha-4137a2232/

Facebook:
https://www.facebook.com/buckaroobuddha1111

Instagram:
https://www.instagram.com/buckaroobuddha1111/

"Gratefulness is a magic tool that will shift the vibrations of your circumstances to what's best for your highest good. It can be in any form big or small. It comes from within your true self."

~ April Kaiser

CHAPTER 19

HAWK EYES

THE AWARENESS YOU NEED TO LEAD

Laura Di Franco, MPT, Publisher

My Story

"Oh shit!"

No one else was in the car, and no other cars were on the road when I swerved across the double yellow lines. The hawk came from the trees on my right and swooped down toward my windshield before flying off to the left.

The excellent reflexes from fourteen years of martial arts training came in handy. My body performs at peak levels, even for everyday moments like this. I was okay physically, but my mind had a field day.

Are you paying attention, Laura? You're on track. Let go. Surrender. Stop worrying. Was this sign good enough?

"Fuck you," I said out loud, trying to catch my breath. And then, I laughed for the next five minutes as I drove to class.

Just the day before, the request in my living room went something like, "Show me a sign I can't ignore."

My healer coaches say you can be a bit demanding with the Universe and your Spirit guides sometimes. I never felt like that was very respectful, but I guess one has to ask for what they want! I certainly needed some practice with that after a life of people-pleasing. Recovering good girl here. Anyone?

Dr. Stephen Farmer's *Animal Spirit Guides* is sitting on my side table. I use it almost every few days when the Spirit world talks to me in the form of animals. Hawks and other big birds have been signs for me for a long time. I'm not sure when that started.

I love birds, all of them. I always have. There's a feather tattooed on my left forearm with the initials YFIB (Your Fear Is Boring). I needed a post-divorce reminder. I wanted the birds and the reminder to be with me every day. The tattoo hurt like hell. I'm not one of those tattoo-addicted people. You won't see me with another one any time soon.

The reminder, though, is to go for the joy. I've been reminding myself for the last eight years, consistently, as a practice, in lots of different ways.

Joy is the ultimate sign I'm on track. The hawks help, and they show up a lot.

"Ah! Look up!"

I shouted to my sister as we walked, turning back toward her with some furious finger pointing, almost losing my hat in the process.

"Do you hear it? That's a hawk!" I craned my neck back to find it soaring in the middle of the bright blue winter sky. It called about ten times in a row.

"What do you think it's telling us?" My sister paused on the trail about ten paces behind me to look up.

"Everything is going to be okay. You're on track. You're on the right path," I said. "They've been around to give me that message for a while now."

I flash to myself in high school, in a stranger's bathroom at a party my friends brought me to. Staring in the mirror at my feathered hair, I leaned over the counter and sniffed up a line of coke. The boyfriend's brother was a drug dealer, and I was a very insecure, introverted loner. The drugs helped me lose my inhibitions, until they got in the way of my soccer career. Thank

God the peak performer in me overpowered the not-good-enough part. I'm grateful for my drive and ambition as an athlete every single day. If it weren't for my body awareness and my love of what's possible, I'm not sure where I'd be today.

You've come a long way from that day, the voice whispers.

Everything you've been through has helped you become who you are now. It's okay. It's time to let go of the shame. It's even time to let go of the drive to push your body to the limit. It's okay to slow down.

Not yet, I thought in reply.

My sister and I continue to hike along the trail in deep conversation about our lives, where we've been, and what's happening now. "We have good genes," she says. We're interested in the DNA that created our high-achieving bodies. Each of us has been a marathoner, and she, an experienced yogi; I, a third-degree black belt. Being in our bodies has been the foundation of the awareness and the secret behind mastering the language of our souls.

Deep awareness has always been a gift between my sister and me. And deeper conversations, connection, and understanding, even when we were living 5000 miles apart, were always present. Now that we're living five miles from each other for the first time in almost 30 years, I struggle with my awareness practice.

What's wrong with you? Why do you feel so uncomfortable?

I think this, but already know why. I'm asking myself the questions I'm afraid to answer.

Your fear is boring, I hear.

"Fuck you!" I say to that wise voice, again laughing out loud. Don't you love that Source has a wicked sense of humor?

The problem with tattooing something on your body that stands for something is that the reminder pops up, even when you don't want it to.

The awareness I've practiced in the last decade of my life means a lot of things to me. It's a survival mechanism, a business coach, a relationship counselor, and above all, a deep knowing and inner wisdom I now trust more than most people I know. There's nothing wrong with people. It's just that no other person will ever know what's aligned for me, so I've learned to take people with a grain of salt. In some cases, I take them with the whole container.

Whether that awareness comes in the form of a hawk, other animals, flickering lights, repeating numbers, the a-ha in someone's words, or the download moving through me to the page, my channel is open, and I don't plan on closing it again. But this day, I'm thinking: *I'm ready to move to the Caribbean and sell coconuts. I'm done.*

With awareness, we have a choice.

And with awareness, sometimes the choices are painful. Today I feel the world conspiring against me in so many ways, making me afraid, again, to take the risks I know will catapult me toward my dreams.

What do you want, Laura?

I like that question, but I'm tired.

I thought I figured that out already, I plead in reply.

Recent circumstances are creating self-doubt and confusion.

You know the self-doubt and confusion are a "no;" you teach people this!

The wise voice is annoying me. Annoyance, I've learned, is a form of resistance in me. I recognize this as one of the signs, the secret internal language I pay attention to.

I choose to leave this one for the next life, I think. *I'm tired. I'm done,* I repeat.

I've learned to observe myself and my life like a hawk. I've learned to take that birds-eye view, soar higher, and take in a bigger picture. I've learned to be aware that I don't know the whole big picture most days and to trust there is one.

I've learned that to help others (anyone), you must model a certain level of awareness. These ninja moves of mindset and awareness help me lead others to their own wisdom. It's my practice of awareness that makes me a leader. And that's the reason I can't give up.

I want to be that leader. I don't want to give up. I talk with the wise me and tell her I'm in it for the long haul. But I do ask for a vacation.

It might be a conversation I don't want to have, or brave words I want to share (in a good way, like saying "I love you") that scare me. It could be a request that feels bold, or saying the sacred "no" to maintain boundaries that keep me healthy. In any of the ways I start to feel that feeling, I know that if I don't address it, the Universe will continue to bring it to the forefront of my life until I pay attention and deal with it.

Sometimes she sends hawks to my windshield.

"Fuck you, Universe!"

Okay, well, maybe not "Fuck you," but seriously, haven't I done enough this round?

Do you all know that saying that "they" tell you when things suck that goes something like: "God won't give you anything you can't handle?" I call BS on that. There are a lot of circumstances in life that people don't handle well or can't handle at all. There are so many things I've been through that showed me what I was made of, and also events that showed me where I fall short. Some days I'm happy to have just survived the moments without killing anyone, or giving up.

Why is life so easy? Why is everything turning out for the best?

The *why* questions were a little tool I picked up from Dr. Noah St. John's book, *Millionaire Afformations.* He turned affirmations into afformations by putting the statements into question form because our brains are wired to solve problems. When I first started writing, recording, and listening to them, I felt goosebumps. The difference between making statements I half believed (affirmations) and asking questions (afformations) was palpable. I felt the shift like when the final puzzle piece slides effortlessly into its place with a touch of one finger.

Why is this resistance in me about talking to my family about the discomfort I feel being around them dissolving so easily?

I taste the feeling inside. I like it. It's not too bitter. It's not difficult. So I try it again, slightly differently.

Why is this feeling of dread about talking to my family disappearing as I speak?

I trust that my inner wisdom will sort it out. And as I write and speak these words and stare out the sliding glass doors at the patio, a tiny little fuzzy-headed grey puff-ball of a bird lands on the chair back, hops to the ground, makes another hop a foot closer to the window, and looks up at me for at least five seconds before hopping away.

Hey there, Laura; you got this. You're on the right track. I love you.

With a small, closed-lipped smile, I close my journal, filled with purpose, release the dread, and get on with something way more aligned: The joy.

I use writing as an awareness practice. It's my main medicine and modality of self-development, along with body awareness meditation practices that I use sitting, walking in the woods, in the bath, and at my desk. Writing is my main channel, and when I connect to my body, stay present, and allow myself to gently move from a ruminating mind to a neutral, more peaceful zone, the writing usually comes fast and furiously. Many times, poems come out. This one about self-love changed how I viewed my self-care practice as a leader.

How Deep is Your Love?

By Laura Di Franco

I think my love goes deep.

And when it seeps back to me

in rings of grit

staining my skin and soul

I sit in wonder.

But, really, is it any wonder?

I think that love is for others, first.

And sure,

loving them is very good,

but not quite as great

as the state of deep love

I shower on myself.

When I keep it running longer

making others wonder

when I'll come out

and if I saved any for them

only then. . .

. . . only *then* is when I know

it's deep enough.

Because the deep love I give to me

is the roots of the tree

that feeds everything

and everybody else.

I will only grow as high

as those roots are deep.

So, today I plant the seed

worship the sun

nourish myself with love

give my roots enough time

to find their way to the core

a place I'm sure

they'll never be unearthed.

Grounded, centered, and strong

in that place

that love

that knowing

that solid foundation

Is where it all begins.

Is today your beginning?

How deep is your love?

It's not about taking care of yourself. It's about how you love yourself, said the wise voice.

Get your food right, do the exercise, take the forest baths and the lavender essential oil ones too, but remember to love on yourself by always soaring high, staying aware, and loving yourself fiercely, first. You get to come first. It's okay.

So, just like how I used my body as the channel throughout my entire life as an athlete, whether it was on the soccer field, running marathons, or sparring with my opponents in Tae Kwon Do, I pause to connect today in that place that knows, my body-mind. I watch her like a hawk.

Today's sacred place is quieter. She can sit still much longer. And when I give myself permission to surrender, I lay back in it like an inner tube down the lazy river at The Bellagio. It's a free-flowing, sun-shining, pina-colada-sipping, glitter-sparkling, bask-in-the-joy kind of feeling.

I'd like to help you write your way there. That's the place you'll live, thrive, and lead from as you evolve into who you were born to be.

The Medicine

WATCH YOURSELF LIKE A HAWK:
HOW TO USE WRITING AS AN AWARENESS TOOL

This whole chapter was channeled. It's being edited and proofed, but the rough draft happened within about 45 minutes, where I breathed first, cleared my mind, and got out of the way of the message meant to move through.

That is some writing badassery. I want you to get to know your connection at that level, too. I want you to trust that the message is there whenever you choose to connect.

What you need:

A timer

A notebook

A pen

STEP ONE: CONNECT TO YOUR BODY

Practice paying attention to your breath for five minutes. Set a timer, get comfy, and begin. Relax, soften, and release with each exhale. Breathe deeply into the pelvic bowl and expand your ribs out on all sides, front and back. Feel everything. Remember, you have feet. What do you notice in terms of sensations? Be curious. Observe by feeling. Do thoughts come? Observe your thinking without attaching to the thoughts. Don't allow a thought to distract you from the sensations in your body. If it does, bring yourself back. Practice this until the timer goes off.

STEP TWO: WRITE YOUR HEART AND SOUL OUT

Grab your pen and notebook and set a timer for five minutes. Fill in the blank: I feel _____. Write as fast as you can without censoring yourself. Don't worry about punctuation, grammar, or even finishing sentences. No rules; just write. Allow the message moving through you to come through the pen to the paper.

STEP THREE: WRITE TO UNDERSTAND YOURSELF

Grab your pen and notebook and set a timer for five minutes. Fill in the blank: The resistance in me feels like _____. Write as fast as you can without censoring yourself. Don't worry about punctuation, grammar, or even finishing sentences. No rules; just write. Allow the message moving through you to come through the pen to the paper.

STEP FOUR: WRITE TO CLAIM YOUR DREAMS

Grab your pen and notebook and set a timer for five minutes. Fill in the blank: If there were no one left to offend, upset, or disappoint, I would _____. Write as fast as you can without censoring yourself. Don't worry about punctuation, grammar, or even finishing sentences. No rules; just write. Allow the message moving through you to come through the pen to the paper.

STEP FIVE: WRITE TO MANIFEST YOUR DREAMS

Grab your pen and notebook, and this time, take as much time as you need to reverse-journal the last bit of writing you did. Read the Step Four writing out loud to yourself. Then, write as if you're living your dream now. Start with this: I'm so happy and grateful now that _____.

No rules; just write. Allow the message moving through you to come through the pen to the paper.

Lastly, what are you feeling? What did the prompts bring up for you? Which felt good? Which felt some other way? Notice everything. Watch everything like a hawk. Notice what is there to teach you and what's there to help you help guide others to *their* inner wisdom.

BONUS STEP FOR MY LEADERS

Create a blog or social post from one of the prompts and share it. Your words change the world when you're brave enough to share them. Lead from joy. Lead from awareness. Lead from love.

Laura Di Franco, CEO of Brave Healer Productions, is an award-winning publisher specializing in business strategy for holistic health and wellness professionals ready to become bestselling authors. She has 30 years of expertise in holistic physical therapy, 14 years of training in martial arts, and her company has published over 54 Amazon bestselling books. The community is over 500 authors strong, and the mission is to wake the world up to what's possible.

Laura is a spoken-word poet, inspirational speaker, and lover of dark chocolate. She has a contagious passion for helping you share brave words that build your business and leave your legacy. Want some advice about your book idea? Schedule a chat with our publishing team! BraveHealer.com

Connect with Laura:

https://www.Facebook.com/BraveHealerbyLaura/

https://www.Instagram.com/BraveHealerProductions

https://www.Twitter.com/Brave_Healer

https://www.linkedin.com/in/laura-di-franco-mpt-1b037a5/

https://www.youtube.com/c/BraveHealerProductionswithLauraDiFranco

"With awareness you have a choice. Choose love."

~ Laura Di Franco

CHAPTER 20

STANDING IN MY POWER

DO NOT MISTAKE DIVINE LOVE FOR WEAKNESS

Seth Rohrer

My Story

"We are starting to feel very much like, is Dad in a good mood today, or is he going to come home drunk and beat us?" I said as I sat across from my Deputy Chief of Operations at the fire department and looked him in the eyes.

"I take offense to that, because I don't drink," he replied with a slight chuckle and a smile on his face.

"Or is Dad going to come in angry and spank us for no reason? I grew up with a father who would spank first and ask questions later. He struggled with health issues, and he is a different man today. But it wasn't okay then, and it isn't okay now," I continued, as I turned to the fire chief to emphasize the point.

There are moments in your life when you must make a choice—stand up to the tyrant in your life or allow yourself to be mistreated. A tyrant is defined as any person in a position of power (or perceived power) who exercises power oppressively or unjustly. This tyrant may be someone around you in your world or your own pattern of thoughts that break you down and keep you from experiencing the amazing truth of who you are. And sometimes this tyrant mistreats others more than you.

In the Toltec teaching, it's not the place of one man to free another from his tyrants, regardless of whether they are internal or external. This is similar to the idea of freeing a butterfly from its chrysalis or a bird from its egg—you rob them of the opportunity to grow strong enough to fly.

We're all the authors of our own beautiful story of life, and every story is purposeful and beautiful, as it's an expression of the divine mother. You cannot know the intent of another's story from your finite perspective. When you interject in another's story just because it looks uncomfortable or painful to you, you may be robbing them of the opportunity to build the mental and spiritual strength to fly into higher levels of awareness.

However, we're still faced with the choice from time to time. Do I stand up to the tyrant or dismiss them and move on?

I was presented with one of these opportunities as a captain in the fire service. We hired a new deputy chief (this DC oversaw all emergency operations in the department) a few years before, and he came with a reputation that most were dreading. It's my practice to dismiss rumors and gossip and observe objectively for myself.

During his brief time with the department, several stories came to my ears about his intimidating, bullying, and demeaning ways with people in and outside of my fire department. I did my best to stay out of the drama and dismiss the gossip. It didn't pertain to me and wasn't my story—until that all changed.

I show up at work the same way I show up everywhere in my life, with unconditional divine love and compassion. People who don't understand unconditional love tend to misunderstand. Also, it's not a common way of being in the fire service.

Do not mistake my love for weakness. This divine love is my power!

This DC informed the Battalion Chief (the BC oversees one of three rotating shifts) that he intended to "break up my crew at Station 81." He ordered my BC (in writing) to move me to another station away from my crew. This violated my contractual rights, so I took the proper steps to overturn his decision. When it made it to the ears of the Fire Chief (the big cheese in charge), he kiboshed this idea immediately.

Now for the real choice. I dealt with this assault on my crew and me, but I had to choose whether to leave it at that or stand up to the bully and call him out for the harassment. I observed the morale in the department steadily declining, while fear grew over the years since this DC was hired. Firefighters began to retreat into themselves and withdraw from projects and special teams to avoid getting in trouble or finding themselves on his radar.

Enough was enough. This DC skated by due to the fear of careers and future promotions being affected. I didn't have the fear. He woke the sleeping giant, and it was time to stand up to this man and send the message that his behavior was unacceptable and unwelcome.

I pursued a meeting with the powers that be, and parties involved for the opportunity to see this situation through his eyes, look him in the eyes, and speak my truth.

The Chief agreed to schedule this meeting within a week or two of asking, so there I sat at the table with my harasser, his boss, and a few others. I created the opportunity to call the darkness out of its hole and into the light. It had nowhere to hide.

Now we find ourselves back where this chapter started—looking the tyrant in the face as I called him out on his abusive and unacceptable behavior in front of his boss, peers, and subordinates.

"I'm seeing guys running scared. They're dropping out of teams and special projects because they no longer want to be under the microscope. They're afraid of getting yelled at. I've witnessed people get yelled at and heard stories of people getting yelled at. That's intimidation and bullying, and it says right in our harassment policy that these tactics will not be tolerated."

With no attempt to deny the claims of intimidation, the deputy chief responded, "Why are you bringing up these other situations? We're here to talk about you."

It's interesting how much can be said in a space where no words exist, especially when dealing with someone who is out of integrity and attempting to miscreate with lies. People who exhibit narcissistic behaviors will attempt to gaslight, belittle, redirect, distract, intimidate, and use any other means to manipulate you and the situation to fit the lies they use to mis-create their story of life and distort the story of others.

As I sat and listened to this man attempt to shift blame onto his subordinates and deny any wrongdoing or missteps, it was clear there would be no impeccability or personal responsibility from his side of the table. The back peddling and attempts to miscreate a story that absolved him of guilt were transparent.

He was careful to use keywords that stop debates in their tracks. Every culture, community, and industry has them. In this case it was, "My main concern is safety." In the love and light community, I hear, "I just don't vibe with that," or "That doesn't feel like it's in alignment." While these are legitimate statements when used sincerely, they're by nature impossible to argue with when used to disrupt a conversation that someone no longer wants to be a part of for whatever reasons.

Even with picture proof that this DC was allowing and taking part in the same 'unsafe' activities he claimed to be so important that he ordered me to be removed from my crew, he continued to spew his bullshit.

"This is also about fair and equitable treatment, and it's not being fair and equitably applied across the board," I pointed out.

"Seth, what do you need here?" asked the Fire Chief.

"I've heard a lot of excuses here, but nothing that really makes sense as to why this happened. When my BC brought the list of concerns originally, the only two legitimate concerns were addressed and corrected."

"Have I said anything since?" the DC retorted.

"Right, because we made the correction, but we made the correction, and my BC was ordered to move me anyway. So, if it's about safety, why was he ordered to move me anyway?" I shot back.

"All I expect is for my people to make decisions. I know that sometimes they're going to be wrong," the Fire Chief interjected.

"Absolutely, but guys are getting yelled at for making decisions and doing exactly what they've been told for years. Make a decision, and if it's not right, we'll coach you on it. That's not what has been happening anymore," I informed the Chief.

"I would like to see us have something productive come out of this meeting. What's something productive we can come out of this with?" said the Chief.

"What I would like to see is for people to quit getting intimidated. To me, it was an intimidating move. I got the power, and you don't. I'm seeing intimidation happen with guys getting yelled at for trying to take the initiative. When they are being yelled at, that's intimidation, and that's violating our policies. It's been going on for a few years, and it's not getting corrected. I want to see that corrected. I want to see guys no longer being afraid to take the initiative and stick their necks out on the line in this department. How do we do that? There is only one common denominator in all these situations, so how do we deal with him?"

I continued, "Chief. I love you to death, and I've been so grateful to work for you for these last 14 years. However, this isn't a new problem, and I know these problems have been landing on your plate over the last few years. What do you do differently now than what's been done over the last few years? As the DC said. If the problem is being addressed and there's no change, what do we do differently to change it?"

This meeting ended with no real resolution, but the Chief was going to consider the information and go from there. A few months later, the Chief told me there was no real repercussion from his end due to what he felt was a lack of tangible reasons. He sent the DC to yet another leadership training course, which had no lasting effect in the past. It was time to go to the next level, the Human Resources Department.

I filed my harassment claim with HR, and this started a domino effect in the department. The Union filed a vote of no confidence and members who had previously been too afraid to speak up began to come forward with written complaints to add to the Union's evidence.

Ultimately, the outcome is not as relevant as the fact that I chose to make a stand, and my choice empowered others to stand up for themselves. It wasn't, and never will be, my intention to cause harm or get retribution. My intention was to stop the mistreatment of my fellow firefighters and myself.

Whether the tyrants stay or go, you must stand in your power, look them in the eyes, and say, "That's not acceptable here." They do not need to physically leave for you and those around you to grow your courage and shine your light bright.

Once you do this, the tyrant is stripped of their power, and I believe for that reason they'll leave, one way or another. Those who seek to steal the light from others will always move on, whether by force or choice, when they lose the ability to do so.

The dark cannot exist in the light because the dark is in and of itself a lie. Lies cannot withstand the truth. Love is the truth and the light that drives out the dark from every corner of your life and consciousness. The brighter you shine your light, the more you run the dark energy out of your reality and your beautiful story of life.

Love is not the emotion you feel for another being. Love is the energy that runs through you and all of life. It's the compassion that resides inside you for all of creation and the common thread that runs throughout the universe.

You are divine love; love is light, and the light is God's presence in all creation. God is in you, and you are in God. We're all unique points of view of the one Source of all creation. When you express your love more completely and shine your light even brighter, you elevate the vibration of the one consciousness connecting us all as one mind and one dream of planet Earth.

How do I cultivate and grow my divine love, light, and power?

This question will change your life and create a beautiful story of Heaven right here on Earth for you and the entire planet, and it's the core of our purpose here during this lifetime.

The Medicine

The pursuit is to remember and embrace your authentic divine loving self and unlearn all the misinformation between your mind and your true essence. Your power lies within, and it always has. Face the tyrant within yourself and those outside of you will have no choice but to retreat. Take back your sovereignty. Reclaim your freedom. Remember your power. You are a powerful being of infinite possibility.

I want to share a very powerful practice I found in a book I highly recommend, *Love Yourself Like Your Life Depends on It,* by Kamal Ravikant.

This was one of my first self-love practices and was an incredibly impactful step in my evolution and elevation. We've programmed self-destructive thoughts due to the example set for us by the well-meaning people in our lives and the words and actions of the misguided, and we've developed the habit of repeating them to ourselves many times every day.

Freedom comes in discovering that you're not your thoughts. You're the thinking of your thoughts, so you can stalk your thoughts by putting your attention on them and observing them. When a self-destructive habitual thought loop comes up, you can choose to alchemize that thought and transform it into words that raise you up.

You can also be proactive and begin to create new habits and patterns by introducing thoughts that will program your subconscious with more powerful words that will create a more beautiful story, end the needless suffering, and send the tyrant packing.

You've been looking in the mirror and being your own tyrant most of your life. *You're too fat or too skinny; your hair's too straight or too curly. Your lips aren't big enough or too big. Your eyebrows are too big or too small. Your face is too round or too skinny. Your ass is too big or too flat.*

Does it feel uncomfortable to say these things to yourself? Is it like old shoes falling apart and not supporting your feet properly, but you hang onto them because they feel comfortable?

At least once a day, if not more, find a quiet room with a mirror, no distractions, and no one around you. I use the bathroom while I'm shaving in the morning. Look deep into your own eyes and say, **"I love you."**

Repeat this to yourself a minimum of ten times and do your best to also feel gratitude for yourself and your body while you say these words.

If you want to see even greater results, do this three times a day. It takes less than five minutes to perform this act of love for yourself, and if you can't commit to 15 minutes out of your day to shift your subconscious thoughts to create more peace and love in your life, please give this book to someone who is ready to step into their power and take responsibility for their happiness.

It's time to choose you. It's time to choose love. Do this because you are love, and you're ready to be the hero of your story that experiences the joy, peace, and connection you were always meant to embody. Commit to this practice for at least two weeks.

I encourage you to stop every time you see your reflection on any surface and think or say out loud, *"I love you."* But at a minimum, once a day, repeated at least ten times in the mirror.

I love you, I love you, I love you, I love you, I love you, I LOVE you, I love YOU, I LOVE YOU, I **LOVE** YOU, **I LOVE YOU!**

Check-in with yourself as you do this. How does this make you feel inside? No judgments. Just check-in. Does it feel uncomfortable? Does it feel soothing? Comforting? Is it challenging to look yourself in the eye? I encourage you to journal what you see and feel each day as you do this practice. This will allow you to see the shifts over time and is a great way to process and move energy.

It's time to become your greatest cheerleader. It's time to evict the tyrant. It's time to stand in your power and show the world that unconditional love will not be mistaken for weakness. It is in fact where your true power and freedom are found.

All my love.

Seth has spent countless hours in his pursuit of love, service, and wisdom. His spiritual journey is one of heart. His mission is to help people shift their awareness and level of consciousness, so they can transform their lives and step into their unique gifts and cosmic power. His nearly 20 years in the fire service in various leadership, mentorship, and instructional roles gives him a unique perspective and ability to guide you through intense inner work to discover, accept, and shine the light on the shadows and heavy energy in your body to reclaim your power and create a beautiful story of Heaven during your time here on Earth.

Join Seth and his wife Angel for a journey to the ancient city of Teotihuacán, Mexico, the magnificent sites of the Sacred Valley and Cusco in Peru, the Great Pyramids of Egypt, and more to be guided on your path to rediscovering the truth of who and what you are. As Master Healers and practicing shamans, Seth and Angel assist you in reclaiming your power, focusing your intent, and creating a life and inner state of being once thought impossible by most people.

As you walk your path through all that currently holds you back, you are not alone. Inner work does not mean lonely work. Seth invites you to join the Bytes of Light Den, where you will find love, support, and assistance as part of a collective that celebrates your awakening to new gifts, applauds newfound awareness beyond the 3D, and encourages you to bring your fears into the light of our safe container.

If you are ready for more focused one-on-one work, Seth would be happy to assist you in rediscovering your inner power and your personal truth.

Join Seth on social media and check out his website to see how he can be of higher service to you in further creating your beautiful story of life.

Connect with Seth:

Instagram: Instagram.com/bytesoflight

Facebook: facebook.com/bytesoflight

Website: rohrerrevolution.com

"Do not mistake love for weakness.
This divine love is your power."

~ Seth Rohrer

CHAPTER 21

HEALING DESPITE THEM

THE FINE BALANCE BETWEEN FUCK YOU AND THANK YOU

Angel Rohrer

My Story

It starts within

It is an internal game.

My own warrior stands watch.

I surrender to my warrior within

I surrender to that part of me.

that knows how to hold.

I lay my head in his lap.

Knowing I am held.

I am loved.

I am my own queen.

Curled up in my furry blankets,

allowing the cool breeze to caress my face.

The cosmos humming the tune of the great Mother.

As I lull myself to sleep, dream, love.

Dream the sparkliest dream!

Your unique ray of light

deserves to shine from the heavens.

Permeating life and dancing with the stars

Holding hands with the love of your life within

I allow myself to surrender and be held.

By the warrior within.

"You are not special!" she yells at me.

Laser beams shoot out of her eyes into my shattered heart as her poison drips into my cells. I recoil from the blast of her energy as it leaks and sinks into the corner where my inner child is hiding. I bring my full attention and protection to that space upon recovery, but it's too late. That arrow was a direct hit into my inner child's heart.

I gasp for air, physically convulsing like the computer inside my brain has just been reset. My nostrils flare with the fierceness of my warrior as I meet her glare with matched intensity. *Who the fuck do you think you are?* I glare wordlessly into the depths of her soul.

That was the beginning of the end of my relationship with that teacher.

I say beginning. Those of us who've struggled with being in a relationship with humans who choose subjugation over empowerment will understand. It takes a great amount of energy to leave abusive relationships, especially when you've been programmed to give your power away to that person.

Yes, they program us.

The skilled ones blanket their manipulation with, "Always give credit to your teacher," over and over. "Make sure you say where the information comes from when you start teaching." Yes. We learn that in school, right? References are a thing.

But when you find yourself saying, "So and so says this," every second sentence, it's time to bring awareness to how deeply you're being programmed.

**There is a balance between honoring the teachings that are passed down
and giving your power away to the teachings.**

Mastery is formed by embodying and integrating the information, owning and birthing your own language and the way to share teachings or your own medicinal art. It's formed with critical thinking and discernment about what serves you and what parts need to be let go of or transformed. You create internal knowledge within. You choose when you no longer need to reference every thought in your head.

It's part of the evolutionary process of humanity and the art of the sacred rebel.

Aligned and authentic teachers will allow you this process and cheerlead you along your way. You'll find out quickly if the teacher you're working with is aligned with these principles by asking questions and reflecting upon their responses. In my experience with this teacher, I was sharing a mind-blowing experience that had me questioning my sanity and I was asking for help.

**What I did not know at that moment,
was that I dove into a realm she had no access to.
She chose annihilation at that moment.**

But heaven forbid I be an outcast from the community I had finally found. *Now what do I do? Shrink myself?* I have shared all my darkest secrets with these humans, and we are all now trauma bonded to the one in control.

I stayed, against my inner knowing. I stayed, knowing this circle was toxic.

I rationalized with myself: *This is part of the work; this is what we have been taught. Allow yourself to be triggered constantly in these circles so you can bring the traumas to the light and heal them.*

I found myself on my knees one night, rubbing cream into her thighs as she stood silent, and I thought: *What has happened to me? What the fuck am I doing right now?*

I learned the hard way, that certain humans will take advantage of your gifts and siphon your energy from your heart, if you let them.

Hear that again, fixer-pleasers.
Humans will take advantage of you as long as you let them.

For most humans, this is unconscious. They're just going along with their storyline, trying to survive. When they teach awareness and spirituality, there is a knowing.

When someone consciously takes advantage of you, there are many words that humans have creatively produced to label such dark magic and subjugation and for these humans, boundaries and no contact become essential.

This too, was another hard lesson taught to me by the same teacher. I was so entwined within this community, my want to be a part of the unit caused me to abandon myself, go against my inner intuition, and I allowed one of her assistants to take pictures of me, ending with skin and lace booty shorts.

Hundreds of pictures were captured of me running through the woods, playing as she encouraged me to take off more clothes. This was a very empowering experience, where I allowed myself to be seen in ways I've never done before, while several women cheered me on.

Quickly, the dark magic rolled in. "I am jealous of you," rolled off her venomous lips to my jaw-dropped face. Spells dropped as she whispered how often she gazed at my beautiful body for months yet refused to give me the images.

The high priestess holding the container sides with my perpetrator,
and I release myself from the circle.

Yet, I still was not done. I still didn't have enough energy to maintain the boundaries, as all my assault traumas resurfaced during this ordeal, and I found myself flailing with no support and spiraling into a mental breakdown. I found myself apologizing to my perpetrator as my energy dropped further and further. I grasped at any support I could find. I had released all my outside friends. All I had was this small circle of humans in my world. Enter my abandonment wounds.

Yes. The shadow work that emerged through the fires of this experience was epic!

Today, I can sniff a perpetrator miles away.
Fuck you.
Your energy is not welcome here.
And thank you.
Go ahead and share this beautiful goddess's pictures with the world.
I dare you.
I have no shame. I have no fear.
Those pictures can only serve to empower me further.

Thank you and fuck you can go together. It's spiritually balanced. I was taught by powerful shamans that all is energy; it's all perception. Some gold came out of this experience. If you think about how you feel when you're in love, your heart pounds, your heart rate increases, and your palms sweat. When you're in fear, your heart pounds, your heart rate increases, and your palms sweat. It's all perception around labeling the emotions racing through your soul basket.

Both can be true as you hold love in one hand and fear in the other.

When an experience like this happens, it takes time to unravel the traumas and energy lines this attaches to. It takes even longer when there is no accountability taken on the other end. When I did reach out to apologize, I was met with, "I was really hurt and this has had far reaching effects, and I don't trust you." That was the final piece that allowed me to release myself from the toxic prison I had created.

I say, "I created," because nobody made me stay there. I had to take radical responsibility for the situation I got myself into, and the humans I allowed within my inner circle. I allowed these humans to treat me this way in the name of healing.

I witnessed myself protecting my teacher, still giving her credit for all my knowledge and hearing other teachers credit her for my gifts as I facilitated energy work on them. "Oh, she has really taught you well!" *Um, no. I came to her with those gifts, mastered already.* Yet I said nothing.

As I stalk energy lines back into my past to find where else I had done that, of course, it made sense. I made excuses and hid the shadow aspects of my marriage for years, covering the abuse I endured, and putting on the white picket fence facade. Here it was showing up again.

Do not gossip about your teacher. Do not share about your circle sisters. You will cause drama. You will be kicked out of the whole community if you tell people what happens in these circles. Nobody will believe you. You are just looking for attention. Remember when so and so spoke out and she got excommunicated?

Grounding into Mother Earth, my roots wrapped around the fiery ball at the center of our planet, I hear the whisperings of Mama Gaia,

Remember love, these were the people that put these dark spells on you:

You are not a writer.

The world is not ready for your gifts.

Your words will not be published in our community.

A small smile creeps across my face as I stand tall, roll my shoulders back, and feel the attachment of my crystalline wings, flutter and stretch to fill the room in full expansion.

Fuck you. And thank you.
Thank you for reminding me to go within,
remember who I am, the energy I house,
and what energy I will never allow into my world again.
I love you and I release you.
Hear me now.
You are released.
And so it is.

244 | BYTES OF LIGHT

There are gold and shadow aspects of all experiences.

The teachings revolve around re-authoring your story to serve you. For me, the gold of working with this woman brought me new teachings, traveling to novel places and having mind-blowing heart-expanding moments in time with myself and others within that circle.

I feel gratitude for the space held while I cleaned out divorce and abandonment wounds, the death of two partners, and a bacterial infection that almost killed me during this whole experience, which had me reeling.

The circle was there for me through it all.
Until I started healing.
Heaven forbid we heal.

All was well, until I started challenging the rules and asking questions and stepping out of the Guru narrative that was programmed within us all. The addiction to suffering was kept alive as the dark energies were permitted to enter the sacred space and dance freely among us.

She did make it clear she struggled with boundaries herself. Another juicy nugget of wisdom drops in clearer.

If someone tells you they struggle with boundaries, believe them.

It's one thing to guess, based off their actions and it's a whole other ballgame when they're up front with their weakness, and you still choose to step in.

Taking radical responsibility for your actions is where the healing begins.

Yes.
I did not listen to my intuition.
I abandoned myself.
I left my inner child unattended.
My warrior left his post.

Challenging her authority, not accepting her coaching style, and speaking my truth about the damaging effects of telling someone they are "not special" brought on a response that shifted me into another dimension.

"I am not your coach; I am your teacher."

I fired the teacher within myself. I put Willow White Wolf in a cage. The programming was so deeply ingrained, I became fearful of repeating my teacher's behaviors as I saw the same addiction to suffering showing up in my circles as I followed her rigid outline of how to run retreats and circles.

It took me years to come back to my own inner coach, the coach who raised hundreds of kids in the gym and preschool. The coach, who adored her babies, lifted them up, and gave them a safe space to shine and grow.

That coach opened Willow White Wolf's den and brought in other expert teachers to heal my inner child and the wolf within.

Healing happens in layers. Honoring exactly where you are in your healing process is important. Sometimes you need to dive right into your rage and hold its hand for the fire to simmer. Sometimes you need to scream "fuck you" into the fire, to help you move through to the other side. Sometimes you can say "thank you" with respect and gratitude and walk away.

Knowing when to leave, honoring your intuition, and disconnecting will ultimately lead to how much energy you need to put into healing yourself after.

The rage does dissipate over time.
And.
This is an important part of the process of letting go.
I choose not to live here.

I choose to go in, touch the wound, acknowledge what's there, apply the medicine, and come back up the root system. You don't have to live in the dark with it. Unhook. Come back to the sunshine and allow yourself to heal.

The Medicine

Sometimes deciding who you are is deciding who you will never be again.

My wish for you is to know love.

I want you to lean into the darkest parts of your soul, hold my hand and walk through the Valley of Death, knowing you are safe.

Knowing the mystery of life becomes your friend when you hold its hand. The great mystery hums a tune you can match and sway with if you choose.

I want you to know the void; knowing this avatar I'm housed in allows you to touch the cosmos, when you draft my energy.

My heart is right here; you're never alone my love.

Understand the gifts of your soul are waiting to be unearthed.

The cracks your heart has experienced allow the light to shine in and heal you from the inside out.

They shine like a prism of love, transforming your heart into the rays of the sun.

Allow the crack open!

Stop trying to hold it all together.

You must disassemble to reassemble.

This is the cycle of life, my love.

Lean into the mother and allow yourself the rebirth you deserve.

Yes, you can reincarnate on Earth in the same lifetime.

Say yes, give yourself permission and allow your wounds to heal.

I have had the honor and privilege of sitting at the feet of many who called themselves 'teachers.'

I have learned a lot through the wisdom that they shared and the trauma I endured, both in my outside world and within theirs.

1. Always do your research on the humans you choose to allow into your inner world, especially if they're giving themselves labels such as teacher, guru, healer, leader, shaman, or elder.

2. Great marketing does not equate to a great teacher. Anyone can pay a professional to beat algorithms. Do not rely on the number of followers to determine your safety within a container.

3. Is this leader inclusive and open to questions that challenge their narrative?

4. Maintain boundaries as you engage and never dismiss your intuition. Use discernment when challenging your own agreements and ask for outside support if you are getting 'red lights' about an experience.

5. Are they saying you need them, or do you need the container they have provided?

6. Know your intent before entering. Do not get distracted by the sparkly 'side gigs.' Remember why you engaged in this community in the first place.

7. Remember, you are your greatest teacher. Do not give your power away and allow someone else to be your only guide.

Angel Rohrer is a former high-performance coach in the power tumbling and trampoline world. She comes with 25 years of National-level experience training athletes of all ages and genders. After retiring, the last ten years were spent focusing her coaching skills in the holistic community, becoming a Crystal Reiki Master teacher and deep tissue massage specialist. She began coaching and healing those looking to wrangle their shadows of life as well as healing their physical body.

Ancient medicine has always been a calling and she spent 30 years mastering breathwork and moving energy with Kung Fu martial arts, as well as apprenticing with the Ruiz family (Author of *The Four Agreements*), Toltec Shamans of the Eagle Knight lineage over the last three years.

She holds hands with the Angel of Death and knows how to navigate darkness with her unique ray of light holding the element of transformation in her soul.

She will commit to you
as deep as you will commit to your own transformation,
walk beside you
as you take that first step into the fire,
so you can shine
your brilliant ray of light.
This is her mission.

Connect with Angel:

On her website: https://www.angelrohrer.com

On her Facebook: https://www.facebook.com/angelrohrer444

On her Instagram: https://www.instagram.com/angel.rohrer/

On her TikTok: https://www.tiktok.com/@angel.rohrer?lang=en

"There is a balance between honoring the teachings that have been passed down and giving your power away to the teachings."

~ Angel Rohrer

CHAPTER 22

SERVICE THROUGH LEADERSHIP

LEADING FROM THE HEART AS YOUR NEW WAY OF LIFE

Angel and Seth Rohrer

As you step into service through leadership and choose to take on the responsibility of holding people's mental health in your hands, you need to understand the immense grounding and responsibility it takes when doing this kind of work.

**You can only teach and hold
to the level you're willing to teach and hold yourself.**

The following excerpt is from a student who was on the front line, in the trenches and advocating for children's lives. The gratitude I have for these warriors of light, true authentic healers, and champions of humanity is immense. This one has had a special place in my heart, and I'm honored to have been a part of their ascension process.

> I know we were asked if we had done the "I see you" exercise,
> to say what we saw in the other person.
>
> Where I struggled, is when I saw some things that I did not
> want to say.

I know nothing is 'good or bad,' just the opposite, but we still label things that way.

When I looked at some people I saw their heart, their wisdom, their warrior, their fire, but in others I saw their longing for perfectionism, their immense guilt, huge pain, etc., and I was not comfortable speaking, truthfully, what I saw or felt. I only wanted to see and say the 'good' things and was not sure how to say the harder ones, the darker ones, so I chose to say nothing at all.

What also stuck out is what you said, that when you see something in another, it is also a reflection of yourself, and *that* has stuck with me, which leads to today. I received an e-mail from a mother who watched one of my presentations. This was a piece of it:

"I too went into postpartum psychosis after the birth of my second child. Unfortunately, my story ends in tragedy as I killed my youngest son four months after he was born. I thought my children were going to be kidnapped, raped, and tortured by an ex-boyfriend, and that this would continue for the rest of their lives. I now am trying to put my life back together, and I so desperately want to make up for what I did when I was sick."

I bawled. First because of the incredible pain and heartbreak I feel.

But the second piece is because of the idea that what we see in others is a reflection of ourselves. That the idea of separateness is simply an illusion of the ego, and we are not separate at all. It is easy to say 'I see you' or 'Namaste' in a yoga class, or a room of like-minded people. Easier to see the similarity when we see the 'good,' the 'light,' and the 'nice.'

Where it is hard is when you see the 'dark,' 'bad,' 'ugly,' and 'hurt' in others and must acknowledge and accept those pieces within yourself and not play into the illusion of being separate.

I would like to think I am above killing my own son.

I would like to think she is psycho, and I was never crazy enough to do anything as horrific. But the truth is, I may have. My delusions were so incredibly real. I do not know that I would not have hurt or killed him. That is incredibly hard to sit with and uncover. To think that I may have done something to my own baby, to know I am not above that.

The only real difference I see between her and me is circumstance and privilege.

I had a family doctor who recognized my symptoms. My professional team knew me personally and had an incredible desire to support me in any way possible, and I had access to the best workers in the country to help me pull through and she did not. The difference is, we simply have different lessons and journeys.

This leads to one of my deepest fears.

I know we can only push others as deep as we are willing to go as leaders. But I find the deeper I go and the more I realize we are not separate, the harder it is to work to truthfully accept myself and others, especially in those places that are difficult, if not completely disturbing.

The ones that are heartbreaking and gut-wrenching to get to and feel almost impossible to sit with, the places driven by fear, chaos, and deep pain.

254 | BYTES OF LIGHT

The places or people I would so desperately want to pretend I was separate from and keep up the illusion as sometimes the illusion is easier to take than the truth!

And part of me wants to just stay in the illusion, but I also believe in the polarity of the world.

To fully understand ourselves we must explore the entirety of our own being.

To fully understand the infinite power of our own light, we must be brave enough to explore every crevice of our own darkness.

But to be honest I am afraid of the dark.

Understand, this is the depths that we swim at and train at. Our mission is to build warriors of light, leaders of this new world we are stepping into where leading by the heart is a way of life.

The authors we have gathered to write in this book have been vetted by us and are considered "safe containers" to do your work in.

There are many dabblers out there causing harm in our communities.

I love that humans are waking up and starting to experiment, however, my mental health requires more than a recreational healer. We provide for you, what we expect to be provided for us. If you choose us as your mirrors, we will expect you to meet us at the depths of your own soul.

The authors in this book, met us and continue to "meet us" at that mysterious place that few choose to travel.

We encourage you to do your homework on who you choose to work with, and we encourage you to start with the authors in this book. The unique rays of light, the different languages, the different tools, they all come from the same source place.

Ultimately, everything you need to achieve the level of consciousness you desire is already inside of you. You are the answer to your own question.

Do not look to others for the answers. Teachers and guides are there to assist you in remembering what you already know in your body and soul.

Look to those teachers that offer to help you find your own truth and not those that attempt to convince you of their truth. The ego will believe it is 'right' and everything else must be 'wrong.' Do not fall prey to this lie. Each ray of light has its own unique perspective.

We're all beings of infinite potential and unimaginable power. No one is above or below another. We are simply at different places on our journey to unlearn and remember our true self.

The real work in this lifetime is to remember that you are love and connected to all of life. This connection brings with it all the knowing you seek and infinitely more. You must unlearn the misinformation given to you that created this false sense of separation and limitation. It's only then that you can remember and reconnect with your true essence, your spirit.

You are perfect because you exist. All that exists is the creation of Source, the Universe, God, or whatever word you choose to represent this life force. All of creation is a beautiful expression of the perfection of life. Your perfection is not dependent on your current situation or circumstances.

Life is love, love is light, and light is all around and inside you. Each one of us is a unique ray of light emanating from the same Source of creation. When you remember that you are light, you regain the ability to shine this light on everything in your world. This is the power to co-create with life itself.

May you too, follow your own unique ray of light, and choose to shine bright for all the world to see.

Join our Bytes of Light Community with Angel and Seth Rohrer on Facebook:

https://www.facebook.com/groups/169323216970027

"You can only teach and hold to the level you're willing to teach and hold yourself."

~ Angel and Seth Rohrer

THE BYTES OF LIGHT

DEN MEMBERSHIP

B.O.L.D is the first and only community of its kind providing a safe and loving space inclusive of all paths to self-empowerment and unconditional love for every soul doing their inner work.

Untangle your roots, open the flow of love and abundance, and take flight to live your wildest dreams so you can go from lonely and confused seeker of truth to the supported, powerful authentic creator of your life.

Bytes of Light Den members receive the following gifts:

- Biweekly live group calls
- Access to a growing library of energetic medicine
- Discounts and early bird pricing for events and retreats
- Discounts on affiliate programs
- Ongoing love and support from the Bytes of Light pack

Follow this link to join the pack:

https://www.rohrerrevolution.com/pl/2147560924

BYTES OF LIGHT

POWER JOURNEYS AND WORKSHOPS

Angel and Seth experience living in the mystery as part of their daily life. As they continue to walk with one foot in one world and the other here on earth, they now share their magic and medicine with others throughout their community and across the world.

Angel and Seth found each other on the pyramid grounds of Teotihuacán, where they committed to their mission of sharing their light knowledge with whoever comes with open arms and is ready to receive. As we know, you can only lead a horse to water. You must be willing to drink the nourishment.

We choose to do retreats as we know the powerful transformation that happens in sacred sites. Experiencing initiations in a group setting and allowing the mystery to dissolve your limited beliefs while you are out of your normal routine, expands your consciousness in the most incredible way. We are guides. Not hand holders. We provide the container for you to do your inner work. There is no better way to grow and expand than through the presence of others, in sacred ceremony, on sacred land.

Join us on our next adventure:
https://www.rohrerrevolution.com/retreats-events

NINA SONGO ENERGY MEDICINE
MYSTERY SCHOOL OF HEALING ARTS

This training is designed to bring you back to yourself and create the life you have always wanted.

This is for you if:

- You are ready to show up for yourself as the fearless warrior and powerful goddess that you are.
- You are ready to break out of the programming you so generously received from those in your life, since birth.
- You are ready to do the work at the deepest level possible for you.
- You are tired of being a victim in your own story of life.

This is not a good fit for you if:

- You are looking for someone to do the work for you.
- You are choosing to allow your fear to keep you stuck and small.
- You are blaming everything and everyone else for your current situation.
- You are unwilling to accept that you have the power within you to change the story of your life.

Sacred initiations, journeys through the chakras, crystal magic, breathwork, and working with the elements are all infused with Toltec, Andean teachings, and a high-performance sports mindset.

ADDITIONAL PROGRAMS

Fire Heart Breathwork

Reiki, Usui System of Natural Healing Certifications

Private Healing Sessions

Dreaming Ceremonies

ACKNOWLEDGMENTS

We would like to express our special thanks of gratitude to our many teachers who have walked this path with us. All humans we encounter have teachings for us. We acknowledge and appreciate the following humans for directing their attention toward us, committing to a path of love and shining their light to help us see clearer, with unconditional love. Jorge Luis Delgado, Lee McCormick, Miguel Ruiz Sr., Jose Ruiz, Miguel Ruiz Jr., Jim Fortin and James Wedmore.

Raeleen Manjak gifted me a golden opportunity to pilot my work within a powerful container she provided. I am very grateful for her strength and tenacity, and her ability to hold and ground me for years, as I navigated my apprenticeships with my Toltec teachers. Thank you for your fierce love and support, Mama Owl. - Angel

Gathering Bytes of Light to come play with us in a collaborative container, was a wild ride in itself. We are humbled to great depths, to play and collaborate with these bright and brilliant souls. With Laura Di Franco as our literary wrangler, we believe this book will provide energetic medicine to heal the collective. Thank you to our Bytes of Light Authors: Laura Di Franco, Jorge Delgado, Kya Dubois, Eliza James, Kristina Dubois, Grace Solaris, Emoke Molnar, Jennifer Falchi, Suzanne Rollen, Rachelle Golding, Dustin Kaiser, April Kaiser, Emily Atlantis Wolf, Daphne Paras, Grace Kohn, and Gurpreet Juneja.

Kya Dubois, my first wolf cub initiate, the holder of many masks, the healer of my daughter wounds, the soul mate to my sister heart, my teacher of mysteries, I love you with everything that I am. Thank you for sharing your light and gifting us with the most precious artwork to emulate the light being infused into this book. - Angel

Seth and I would also like to thank our parents and friends who supported us and challenged us along this journey. All humans come into your world for a reason, whether it be for lessons or love, and we are grateful for it all.

"Your will requires your discipline as you master a new way of life."

~ Angel Rohrer

My husband Rob and I spent the better part of five years working with Angela.

She is a true healer, very intuitive and creative in her treatments. She has been an integral part of my self-care when coping with anxiety and I credit her with helping me get to a point where my anxiety has greatly decreased.

A huge success! She is stubborn and strong. She will find a way to release whatever you are holding on to through grounding, body awareness, energy, and crystal work. She is one of a kind, we highly recommend her!

~ Jessica Niedermayer, Singer/Songwriter, Wild Honey
~ Rob Niedermayer, NHL Hockey Hall of Fame

I have been blessed to have Angel and Seth in my life.

They create and write from a place of deep passion and love for humanity during these times of transformation and transmutation. If you are ready to expand and remove the illusionary veil keeping you trapped in your current reality.

I highly recommend diving into this offering and extract the magic meant for you!

~ Ocean Eagle Best Selling Author and Founder of Activation Breathwork

Angie started coaching me in power tumbling and trampoline when I was about 11 years old. She immediately gave me so much support and encouragement to learn fast and get to higher levels for competitions. She believed in me. During some years I trained with her for 25 hours per week. Not only was she an amazing coach in the gym, but she ended up acting like a big sister to me, coaching me through hard life lessons and holding me while I cried. It was evident that she genuinely cared for all her athletes. My family was going through some challenging times and Angie took me in and cared for me like we were family. She was always a strong figure in my life; I looked up to her and loved being around her. Now years later, to see her on this path of healing is no surprise. Angie has always been deeply intuitive, empathic, and nurturing. She has been a true angel in my life along with countless others. It only makes sense for her to continue healing and sharing her gifts.

"Love fearlessly, time and time again. There's no better feeling in the world."

~ Kristina Engel, R.Ac

Made in the USA
Coppell, TX
21 June 2023

18377497R10164